Farewell to Schools ? ? ?

edited by

Daniel U. Levine

University of Missouri, Kansas City

and

Robert J. Havighurst

University of Chicago

Charles A. Jones Publishing Company
Worthington, Ohio

Contemporary Educational Issues
National Society for the Study of Education

Farewell to Schools??? Daniel U. Levine and Robert J. Havighurst, Editors

Models for Integrated Education, Daniel U. Levine, Editor

Accountability in Education, Leon M. Lessinger and Ralph W. Tyler, Editors

PYGMALION Reconsidered, Janet D. Elashoff and Richard E. Snow

Reactions to Silberman's CRISIS IN THE CLASSROOM, A. Harry Passow, Editor

2 3 4 5 6 7 8 9 10 / 76 75 74 73

Library of Congress Catalog Card Number: 75-184316
International Standard Book Number: 0-8396-0015-1

Printed in the United States of America

Series Foreword

Farewell to Schools??? is one of a group of five publications which constitute the first of a series published under the auspices of the National Society for the Study of Education. Other titles are:

> *Accountability in Education*, edited by Leon M. Lessinger and Ralph W. Tyler
>
> *Reactions to Silberman's CRISIS IN THE CLASSROOM*, edited by A. Harry Passow
>
> *Models for Integrated Education*, edited by Daniel U. Levine
>
> *PYGMALION Reconsidered* by Janet D. Elashoff and Richard E. Snow

For more than seventy years the National Society has published a distinguished series of Yearbooks. Under an expanded publication program, beginning with the items referred to above, the Society plans to provide additional services to its members and to the profession generally. The plan is to publish each year a series of volumes in paperback form dealing with current issues of concern to educators. The volumes will undertake to present not only systematic analyses of the issues in question but also varying viewpoints with regard to them. In this manner the National Society expects regularly to supplement its program of Yearbook publication with timely material relating to crucial issues in education.

In this volume Professors Havighurst and Levine have brought together essays by four critics who have raised serious objections to conventional thinking about the role of formal schooling in contemporary society. These viewpoints on schooling are considered by several writers, some of whom refute the critics while others are supportive.

The National Society for the Study of Education wishes to acknowledge its appreciation to all who have had a part in the preparation of this book.

Kenneth J. Rehage
for the Committee on the Expanded Publication
Program of the National Society for the Study of
Education

Contributors

Carl Bereiter, professor of applied psychology, The Ontario Institute for Studies in Education, Toronto, Ontario, Canada

Amitai Etzioni, professor of sociology, Columbia University, director, Center for Policy Research

Paul Goodman, author and lecturer

Maxine Greene, professor of English, Teachers College, Columbia University

Robert J. Havighurst, professor emeritus of education, University of Chicago

Ivan Illich, director, Centro Intercultural de Documentación, Cuernavaca, México

Philip W. Jackson, professor of education and of human development, director, the Laboratory Schools, University of Chicago

John Ohliger, associate professor of adult education, The Ohio State University

Everett Reimer, coordinator, Centro Intercultural de Documentación, Cuernavaca, México

Mortimer Smith, executive director, Council for Basic Education

Peter H. Wagschal, assistant professor of education, University of Massachusetts

Preface

It has become evident that existing institutional arrangements for raising and educating the young deserve critical reexamination in the light of present and future developments in the societies in which they are embedded. For example, no one can deny that the family in urbanized societies has lost much of its power to exclude outside influences which interfere with traditional socialization goals and practices in the home; it is partly for this reason that more and more of the burden of socialization has been placed on the school. But is the school really the best institution to help the young achieve an authentic identity, personal effectiveness as a citizen, or any one of two or three dozen other tasks which seem to have fallen to the school because other institutions have been forced to abdicate or suitable new institutions have not yet been invented?

Similarly, compulsory public school systems tend to not respond quickly enough, if at all, when called on to adapt themselves to evolving and emerging needs of the young. Precisely because they are responsible for serving all the children of all the people in a complex, bureaucratic society, compulsory school systems sometimes tend to become bumbling bureaucracies in which responsibility becomes too dispersed and displacement of goals begins to favor the interests of employees rather than clients. Can compulsory school systems respond flexibly and appropriately in recognizing the changing pressures and demands on youth, or shall formal schooling be minimized or abolished in favor of new institutions or informal, noninstitutionalized arrangements for accomplishing the purposes of education?

We cannot think intelligently about such matters or respond to them wisely unless we first ask the right questions—a task which will require a tremendous amount of hard thought, diverse experimentation, and careful assessment of results and possibilities. Even though a few educators and laymen have begun to look at the matter in this light, the process of identifying and finding answers to the right questions is still in its infant stages. What are the irreducible tasks of education that must be accomplished to make contemporary society viable, and what should be the school's role, if any, in accomplishing them? Who will be responsible for tasks not performed by compulsory public schools, and what institutions, if any, must be invented to get them done?

To encourage widespread discussion of these matters, and in keeping with its stated purpose to examine the most fundamental issues in education, the National Society for the Study of Education is sponsoring the publication of this volume dealing with the fundamental problem of schooling and deschooling. The format which has been chosen is to reprint four essays which are among the most thought-provoking of the materials now available on the general topic of schooling in contemporary society. The first essay is Everett Reimer's effort to return to first principles in working out systems-analysis perspectives on the role of schools and the meaning of education in society.* Next, an essay by Carl Bereiter inquires whether the goal of compulsory schooling may be fundamentally unrealistic simply because of the problems of obtaining effective teachers in sufficient numbers. Paul Goodman, in an excerpt from his book on *The New Reformation*, explains why he believes that learning should occur "incidentally" while participating directly in society outside the school. Finally there is an essay in which Ivan Illich proposes steps he thinks might be taken to make society itself an organized learning environment more effective and meaningful than compulsory schools.

Following this section, seven reactors constitute a symposium to discuss the ideas put forward and the issues raised in the preceding material. Reactors were asked to respond as directly or indirectly as they wished to the essays in the first section and to pursue implications or issues in any directions they thought were suggested by the essays and excerpts. No attempt was made to systematize the symposium responses other than to ensure that the list of reactors included a range of individuals who as a group might be expected to represent a full range of opinions on the topic of schooling and deschooling. The contingencies of the publication schedule made it necessary to ask the symposium participants to return their papers within eight weeks of the time they received copies of the material to which they reacted. The Society is grateful to the reactors for their willingness to participate despite busy schedules and to publishers and authors who gave permission to reprint the writings which comprise the first half of this volume.

Daniel U. Levine and
Robert J. Havighurst

*For a later and more comprehensive statement of Reimer's thinking on this topic, see Everett Reimer, *An Essay on Alternatives in Education* (Cuernavaca, Mexico: Centro Intercultural de Documentacion, 1970).

Contents

Chapter

Responses

I

Proposal for a Planning Seminar Aimed at the Development of Basic Educational Alternatives

Everett Reimer and Ivan Illich

Statement of Purpose

We regard the present school system as requiring basic reform or replacement for the following reasons:
1) Two-thirds of the world's population cannot be afforded education at present unit costs.
2) The school system fails in its attempt to educate most students of the lower class. Most of them drop out before they become literate.
3) The school system also fails in part to educate most of its nominally successful students, stultifying rather than nurturing their lifetime capacity and desire for learning.

Our justification for attempting such an ambitious project is that a plethora of projects of lesser scope show little promise of making a significant impact on the problems outlined above.* In the typical case such projects succeed initially, but, once special support is

---

*The above problems are listed in what we regard as their order of importance, but they are not discussed in this order. Thus, specific reference to economy in education comes late in our exposition.

withdrawn, their influence within the larger system gradually dissipates, leaving no discernible effects upon it. All of these projects assume the validity of the present system, yet the system rejects them almost in the manner of an organism rejecting a foreign substance. Furthermore, no project we know of promises economies of the order required to make education universally available in the foreseeable future. Developing nations, on the other hand, show every indication of placing major reliance for the education of their people on the institutional patterns of the wealthier nations. Perhaps the major hope of avoiding this eventuality is not only to demonstrate the economic contradictions involved but also to illustrate possible alternatives.

We feel it necessary, therefore, to examine the school system in its entirety in the hope of discovering fruitful directions for change.

We feel that we can best describe and justify the seminar method we propose by summarizing the two stages which led to the development of this proposal.

I. Early Background
(Phase I, 1956-1967)

The senior authors of this proposal, Everett Reimer and Ivan Illich, met in Puerto Rico in 1956. Reimer, as executive secretary of the Committee on Human Resources of the Commonwealth, was making an assessment of Puerto Rico's needs for trained manpower and outlining an educational program to meet these needs. Illich was vice-chancellor of the Catholic University at Ponce, a member of the Commonwealth Board of Higher Education, and founded a center for the training of teachers, social workers, and clergy engaged in service to Puerto Rican immigrants to New York City.

Results of the manpower study indicated a need to reduce the number of dropouts from all levels of Puerto Rico's school system. The recommendations to achieve this purpose were well received and fully carried out, but it soon became evident that retention rates were being increased at the expense of grade standards, i.e., that the results of the program to reduce dropouts were illusory. More children were staying in school, but they were not learning more.

In 1962, Reimer moved to the Alliance for Progress, an adviser on social aspects of development, and found the educational problem of Latin America to be an exaggerated version of the Puerto Rican situation.

Half the children who entered school never got beyond the first grade, and half of those who entered the second grade never reached the third. There was every reason to believe that a nominal improvement in these rates would be just as illusory as it had been in Puerto Rico. Manpower calculations showed an even more urgent need to expand education in the rest of Latin America than in Puerto Rico, but cost estimates showed the recommended educational programs to be completely beyond the economic capacities of Latin American countries.

Illich, meanwhile, had shifted his base of operations to Mexico in 1961 and was engaged in training North American volunteers, missionaries, and technical assistants for service in Latin America. In following up the work of his students who went into education, he found that, far from aiding the churches to reach and help the masses of Latin America, most of them were engaged in buttressing the power of the privileged minority by helping to operate a school system which could never hope to reach the masses.

Some of the basic problems of the school system, both public and private, which Reimer and Illich had begun to discuss in Puerto Rico were now seen to be much more general and more basic than had earlier been evident. From 1960 on, a spate of studies on the educational problems of the United States added evidence that some of the basic problems were universal and were merely exaggerated in developing countries by the relative scarcity of resources.

In 1964, Reimer returned to Puerto Rico and, as consultant to Angel Quintero, the recently appointed secretary of education, began to try to cope with the problems of costs and effectiveness of the Puerto Rican public school system, especially with its lack of effectiveness in teaching and retaining the children of the economically underprivileged. This experience, essentially the failure under the most favorable of circumstances to achieve any marked improvements, led to an ever deepening conception of the nature of the problem. Illich, meanwhile, had succeeded in establishing a language training and documentation center (CIDOC) at Cuernavaca, Mexico, which is entirely financed out of tuition fees and which now provides an independent institutional base for Latin American studies, research, and publications. Part of the resources of this center were used in the years 1961-1966 to provoke a major reevaluation within the native and foreign clergy in Latin America (Roman Catholic, Episcopalian, Presbyterian et al) toward the continued use of church-controlled manpower and money in private education.

Both, now convinced by their own experience and by the apparent failure of massive efforts in the United States, decided early in 1967 to attempt a systematic analysis of the school system which began in the summer of 1967 and was continued in an eight-week seminar during the following summer. In Cuernavaca in 1968, from July 15 to September 1, Reimer and Illich met three times a week with Miss Valentine Borremans, director of CIDOC since 1963, and Miss Patricia Cloherty, candidate for the Ph.D. in international education at Columbia University. In addition to attending the meetings, these regular members of the seminar accepted research assignments between sessions. Some sessions of the seminar were attended by others, including Samuel Anderson, professor of psycho-linguistics, Wesleyan University, Middletown, Connecticut; Pierre Furter, UNESCO staff member in Venezuela; Eduardo Rivera, assistant secretary for Planning, Department of Education, Puerto Rico, and Robert W. Allen, specialist on educational games, Nova University, Fort Lauderdale, Florida.

II. Cuernavaca (Phase II, 1968)

Definition of the School System
(Partial Summary of the 1968 Seminar)

The group began by defining the present school system as the institutional union of four social functions:

1) Custodial care: provision for the safety and well-being of children, adolescents, and young adults; to some degree serving *in loco parentis,* and thereby maintaining the dependent status even of persons who are legally adult

2) Selection for social roles and social status: determining and certifying eligibility for progress within the school system and eventually for employment, for the exercise of certain basic rights of citizenship, and for other kinds of social roles and status

3) Value formation: teaching the socially approved values, the non-cognitive goals of education as set forth in Bloom's taxonomy(1)

4) Cognitive Education: provisionally defined in terms of the cognitive goals of education as outlined in Bloom's taxonomy(2)

While we recognize that these social functions can never be wholly separated, we believe that the present form of their institutional union in the school system is largely responsible for the major shortcomings attributed above to this system. Specifically, we believe that these functions are given priority in the present system approximately in the order in which they are listed above and that the relatively low priority thus accorded to cognitive education accounts in considerable part for the high costs and low student achievement characteristic of most schools.

We believe that conflicts among the listed functions also account, in part, for what we regard as the unsatisfactory benefit-cost ratios of schools. For example, the way the selection and education functions are now combined makes school a failure experience, and thus a punishment system, for half the students. Most of the other half are forced to adopt educationally sterile forms of answer-getting behavior in order to avoid the punishment of falling into the left-hand tail of the grade distribution.

Alternatives to the Present School System

In order to guide our planning and to be logically exhaustive, we distinguished three directions which the discussion of alternatives could take:

1) The commercialization of the present functions of the school system, i.e., the marketing of custodial care, selection and certification, indoctrinational, and educational services
2) The redistribution of these functions to nonspecialized agencies, e.g., custodial care to the home, selection to employers, indoctrination to religious groups, education to guilds
3) Radical reform of the present system, i.e., retention of the four functions in one institution but with a reduction in the conflicts between them and with a higher priority for the educational function

We briefly explored these directions by listing the examples of specific alternatives actually available, of which members of the seminar had personal knowledge. In order to do this, we first divided the clientele for the services of the school system into four age groups and social classes. Then we filled out tables like the following:

EDUCATIONAL SERVICES COMMERCIALLY AVAILABLE

	Class :	Upper :	Middle :	Lower Urban :	Lower Rural
Age 2-5	: :	: :	: :	: :	
6-12	: :	: :	: :	: :	
13-18	: :	: :	: :	: :	
19	: :	: :	: :	: :	

The contents of a table like the foregoing, filled out as completely as possible, gave us an overview of the educational services and materials which households of different social class and geographic location could purchase for members of various ages.

Similar tables were filled out for indoctrination, custodial care, and selection, not only for services commercially available but also for those provided by homes, employers, unions, and other noncommercial, noneducational institutions.

From these tables we could make generalizations like the following:

1) Similar educational experiences are available to upper-class children of pre-school age, to middle-class elementary school children and to lower-class high school children, i.e., there appears to be a lag of about six years from one class level to another in the availability of such educational experiences as trips, music, books, or theater of a given kind.

2) Such selection and certification services as tests, advanced placement, and provisional admission are little utilized by the upper class, are seldom at the option of the lower class, and thus serve almost exclusively the upwardly mobile middle class.

3) Individualized services, i.e., tailor-made education, indoctrination, and custodial care, are the prerogative of the upper class, the use of mass-produced services characterizes the middle class, while the lower class, which has only marginal access to mass-produced services, has a range of informal educational opportunities which the other classes do not fully share.

4) All of the functions performed by schools are also available independently, and in almost any combination, either commercially or as functions of noneducational institutions somewhere in the world if not in any one country.

The results of this exercise led us to the idea of empirical surveys which would establish the actual availability, from alternate sources, of the services now provided by the school system. Since part of our planned future work is to outline and detail the proposed content and methods of such surveys, we will refer to them again later in this proposal.

Having briefly explored the potential for commercialization and redistribution of the current functions of schools, we turned to the third alternative of reforming the present system. At this point, we were compelled to be more specific about what kinds of changes would constitute reform. We began by reaffirming our primary interest in education defined as the cognitive development of the individual. We recognize the importance of providing for the general well-being of the young, of selection for social roles, and of the transmission of cultural values, and we recognize that any change in the school system will have to make provisions for the performance of these functions. We do not, however, feel that schools are uniquely qualified to perform these functions or, indeed, that they are designed to perform them very well. Schools are, on the other hand, the only institutions which have ever specialized in the cognitive development of individuals and, at this stage of world history, nothing seems to us more crucial than to try to provide optimum conditions for the development of all men's minds. Thus, even if it should be determined that schools must continue to give priority to functions other than cognitive development, this would require that other institutional means be developed to achieve the cognitive aims of education.

A basic guide from which norms for reform could be derived seemed to be required. We attempted, therefore, to define our concept of education and succeeded not in saying much that is new but, hopefully, in developing a vocabulary general enough to accommodate some conflicting views. We noted, first of all, that much learning is unplanned. Learning directly from nature is unplanned unless the student is deliberately studying nature. Learning directly from the culture, unless it is research, is also unplanned. Not even all planned learning is education. Learning directed toward the performance of nonlearning tasks is better called training. Only planned learning which has future learning as its objective is education as we define it. Our paradigm can be summarized as follows:

LEARNING

1. Unplanned
   A. from nature
   B. from culture
2. Planned
   A. for performance (training)
   B. for learning (education)

Education defined as planned learning implies, at least in the case of young children, a two-person relationship between "teacher" and student. In terms of the commonly held theories of learning, the role of the "teacher" is to select the learning task, to select the appropriate reinforcement schedule, and to supervise the learning process. Since, however, the aim of education is further learning the best education is that which maximizes lifetime learning. A program for lifetime learning can be written only piecemeal, and it appears, intuitively, that the later stages of an optimum program can only be written by the learner himself. One objective of education, therefore, is that the student become his own teacher. The timing and other aspects of the procedure by which the "teacher" role shifts to the student are obviously one of the critical aspects of education.

The content of the educational curriculum can be derived from the goal of maximizing lifetime learning if we accept that all of man's learning tools can be defined as codes, i.e., as ways of encoding sensory inputs. Man's major code is natural language, which in its oral form is learned at home. Encipherments of natural language, such as reading and writing, appear to be the next most important learning tools, basically because they provide those who master them with a secondary longterm memory system which is collective as well as individual. At some future date, computer language may become as important as reading and writing, for similar reasons.

Next in importance, after these encipherments, come the major sublanguages of mathematics, the sciences and the arts, and the major metalanguages such as linguistics, philosophy of science, etc.

Finally, along with code learning and encipherment, several value systems bound up with cognitive learning must be effectively transmitted through formal education. One is the set of values attached to coding and encipherment themselves. Another, less easily specified, is that set of values which maintains the right relationships between facts and values.

The preceding paragraphs define, in a very general and preliminary way, our ideas as to the priorities which should govern a reformed school system.

Possibilities for Economy in Education

One of the problems cited at the outset is that most of the world's population cannot be afforded education at even the lowest cost levels associated with present school systems. It is clear that regardless of other reforms, economies in education must be achieved if the world's masses are not to remain "ignorant," economically and politically impotent and rapidly increasing in number. The preceding discussion provides some ideas of how basic economies might be achieved; others were drawn, less systematically, from the experience of members of the planning group.

Economies must fall into one of the following classes:
1) Reduction in the time required to achieve educational goals
2) Reduction in the unit costs of inputs to the system required to achieve those goals
3) Reduction in the inputs per student or, inversely, an increase in the number of students served per unit input

Under 1), for example, the time required to achieve educational goals can be reduced by:

a) Setting fewer or lower educational goals
b) Setting fewer or lower goals for associated custodial care, selection, or indoctrination
c) Achieving goals more efficiently

Setting fewer educational goals implies reducing the curriculum, which is not only possible but highly desirable on many counts. The typical elementary school teacher today has six subjects to teach, with from six to twelve learning objectives per subject per semester. With thirty students, if individualized instruction is given more than lip service, this teacher has at least 1080 specific learning objectives to achieve per semester, an obviously impossible responsibility as schools are now organized.

Lower educational goals, on the other hand, are not indicated. Goals for the learning of basic codes and encipherments need to be raised to levels which will guarantee use of the skills in question as tools for further learning. This will be feasible only if offsetting economies can be made—if, for example, the number and level of goals for custodial care, selection, and indoctrination can be reduced. This would appear to be possible. Students would probably be better off with fewer hours spent in class, with less elaborate space, with fewer tests, gradings, and sortings, and with less planned value-teaching, most of which is mutually cancelling in today's school situation.

Rescheduling of learning tasks offers other great opportunities for achieving educational goals more efficiently, especially if the lifetime of the learner is used as the base for rescheduling. Adults learn to read, for example, in one-fifth the time it takes to teach children, although children might learn as rapidly if one waited until they were ready or else used different techniques at an earlier age.

Incentives for specific achievement also promise great reductions in the time required for learning. Bonuses for learning to read at a given level of skill, payable to teacher, parent, or pupil, whoever is responsible for the learning, might work well even in the context of the present school system. Daily reading to very young children might be a means not only of earning such bonuses but also of sending all children to school literate.

Reduction in unit costs, the second type of economy cited above, can be attained by substituting lower-paid personnel for professionally trained teachers in the performance of nonprofessional tasks. They can also be obtained by mass-media instruction and by shifting the instructional load from teachers to materials, which are subject to economies of scale.

As an example of the third class of economies listed above, using students as teachers and in other roles of responsibility has a potential demonstrated in the English Lancastrian system and now again in a version of the English primary shcool reform which groups children of varying ages in one learning group. The Lancastrian system achieved pupil-teacher ratios of 250, and such ratios are not inconceivable in a modern system free of the defects of the original.

Enough examples have been cited to make clear that educational economies of very great scope are possible. Whether they are also practicable is to ask what sacrifices they entail and whether strategies capable of securing their successful adoption exist.

Outline of Strategy Variables

In our discussion of strategy, we distinguished four tasks:
1) Identification of the interests served by the existing school system
2) Identification of groups whose interests would be served by changes in the present system and of the motives to which an appeal might be made
3) Identification of relevant beliefs about the present school system
4) Survey of possible tactics

In relation to the first task, we concluded that the present school system serves primarily to insure the succession of middle-class children to status levels no lower than those of their parents. It relieves middle-class parents of all but routine decisions about the future of their children and also relieves them of partial responsibility for their custody. The older generation is also relieved by this school system of some of the impact of the young upon the political process. Older members of the labor force are also partially protected from the competition of the young. Other examples of the interests of specific population groups served by the present school system might only elaborate the general theme stated above, but this cannot be said for certain until a systematic inventory is made of such population groups and the interests relating them to the school system.

Turning to the second task listed above, we decided that positive strategy planning would consist in a similar inventory of such population groups as students, parents, teachers, school administrators, employers, etc., identifying for each which of their interests could be served by replacement or reform of the present school system. The interests of students, as judged by themselves, would be served, for example, by cutting class hours in half or by paying for school attendance and might be served in a variety of other ways. The interests of at least some parents would be served by an increase in the learning rate of their children, by increased enjoyment of school work, etc. Some of the potential interests of taxpayers, employers, etc., are equally easy to identify. The first step in serious, positive strategy planning would be to complete and verify a detailed list of such interest potentials for the significant population groups.

Task three involves another, but parallel, kind of planning concerned with beliefs rather than with the interests of client groups. Most parents, for example, believe that their children learn more as a result of attending school than they actually do. Many employers put more faith in years of schooling as a selection device than is warranted. Most students believe it is harder to learn mathematics or a foreign language than it actually is. A systematic inventory of such beliefs, in relation to their truth value, would suggest another array of tactics comparable to those related to interests.

Task four goes beyond research to the interpretation of research results for action planning. Tactics would follow directly from such an array of strategy potentials as are outlined in the preceding paragraphs. To serve the economic and power interests of lower-class parents, for example, one might propose that an educational account be established for each child at birth from which parents could spend for educational goals and services of their choosing. Such a proposal would also, of course, appeal to the interests of potential purveyors of such goods and services. Offering bonuses for specific learning achievements, assigning teaching roles to children, and expanding the market for direct purchase of professional services by parents from educators are other examples of tactics which suggest themselves as means of appealing to the specific interests of particular groups.

III. Outline of Future Work (Phase III, 1969-1971)

In the planning outlined above, we have obviously done no more than to develop an overview. We have defined the difficulty. We have defined the present school system and, we believe, have discovered the roots of the difficulty. We have shown that various kinds of alternatives to the present system exist. We have defined our objective and have outlined a systematic, strategic, and tactical approach to its realization.

It may be equally important to summarize what we have not done. We have tried to avoid committing ourselves to a theory of learning, child development, or pedagogy. We have also tried to avoid an explicit "world view", i.e., to derive a theory of education from any value other than that of "learning" itself. So long as alternatives to the present school system have lower unit costs, serve more people effectively, and promise more learning over the lifetime of students, we find them acceptable. We believe, further-more, that a variety of alternatives may not only be easier to achieve but may in the long run result in better education than an "ideal" solution.

During the next two years, we plan to do the following:

1) Repeat, more thoroughly, some of the work we have done. We would, for example, survey the literature in an effort to get a more complete and documented listing of the availability, from schools and from alternate sources, of the goods and services now provided by the school system.

2) Carry out the planning outlined above. We would, for example, attempt a systematic analysis of the economic, political, and status interests associated with the present school system and with possible alternatives to it. We would attempt a similar analysis of the beliefs held concerning the present school system and concerning possible alternatives. These analyses would be based upon the knowledge and judgment of partici-pants in the seminar and upon a survey of the literature.

3) Develop tentative designs and recommendations for empirical studies which would discover, from appropriate population samples, respondents' actual sources of educational goods and services, their knowledge of other sources, their beliefs about and their interest involvements in the present school system and possible alternatives to it. Such population samples would probably be stratified not only by age, sex, and social class but also by such functional categories as student, parent, teacher, administrator, taxpayer, employer, etc.

4) Extend our analysis of planned and unplanned learning, training, and education. Pursue the idea of expressing educa-tional objectives in terms of codes, encipherments, and immedi-ately associated value systems. We are not interested in formal theory as an end product but are looking for guides to the im-provement of educational practice.

5) Try to answer, systematically, such questions as the following:

   a) Why does the teacher-classroom-homogeneous student group remain the structural module of the school system?

   b) Why do these modules continue to be organized in ranked layers?

   c) Why do teachers remain the major direct source of instruc-tion?

   d) Why is schooling increasingly regarded as the full-time oc-cupation of youth over an expanding period of years?

   e) Why are schools taking on an increasing number of training functions?

   f) Why do employers give increasing weight to schooling?

We do not believe that such concepts as cultural lag adequately explain these phenomena. We believe, rather, that the answers may lie in as yet unexplored aspects of our functional analysis of the school system. It may be, on the other hand, that this analysis will have to be expanded to include additional functions or otherwise be modified or replaced. We want to work toward a more adequate theory of the school system, not because of any interest in formal theory, as such, but because a better understanding of the system will be an effective instrument for orderly change.

6) Try to define and spell out the essential characteristics and implications of a limited number of alternatives to the present school system. Until this is done, only vague assessments of corresponding availabilities, interests, and beliefs can be made. This task, however, is as difficult as it is important, and we cannot expect more than limited success.

7) Develop specific recommendations for research and for legislative, government-administrative, entrepreneurial, and political action. It is probably not very profitable to try to guess what the substance of these recommendations might be. Possible examples, most of them already referred to in the preceding text, include:

   a) Promotion of schools operated for profit
   b) Transfer of training functions to employers
   c) Educational accounts, e.g. extension of GI-type educational benefits to the general public and to all levels of schooling
   d) Bonuses paid to individuals for specific educational achievements
   e) Concentration on the teaching of coding and encipherment skills
   f) Transfer of the instructional function from teachers to didactic materials
   g) Institutional separation of custodial care, selection, indoctrination, and cognitive education
   h) Taking teachers out of schools and substituting the kind of relationship that exists between doctors and hospitals

These ideas are not original; neither have they been subjected to critical analysis. One purpose of continuing the seminar is to subject such ideas to the critical scrutiny of persons capable of improving them, rejecting them or substituting others, and of promoting the adoption of those ideas which manage to obtain a reasonable concensus.

Ideas can neither be evaluated nor applied, however, in the summary form in which they are stated above. Everything depends, for example, on the kinds of schools which are run for profit, what they teach, who runs them, how they are promoted, and what else is done. A second reason for continuing the seminar is to get such ideas into a shape which makes evaluation and adoption possible. Much depends, also, on whether a set of recommendations constitutes merely a list or a coherent pattern. Our initial and also our closing argument is that only a systematic analysis and an integrated set of recommendations have a chance of coping with the problem. We are obviously not able to make such a set of recommendations on the basis of what we have done to date.

From Everett Reimer and Ivan Illich, *Alternatives in Education, 1968-69* (Cuernavaca, Mexico: Centro Intercultural de Documentacion, 1970). CIDOC Cuaderno No. 1001. An expansion of this essay has been published as *School Is Dead: Alternatives in Education* (Garden City, N.Y.: Doubleday and Company, 1971).

Notes

1. David R. Krathwohl, Benjamin S. Bloom, and Bertram B. Masia, *Taxonomy of Educational Objectives, The Classification of Educational Goals, Handbook II: Affective Domain* (New York: David McKay, 1964).
2. Benjamin S. Bloom, ed., *Taxonomy of Educational Objectives, The Classification of Educational Goals, Handbook I: Cognitive Domain* (New York: David McKay, 1956).

II

A Time to Experiment with Alternatives to Education

Carl Bereiter

The Educational Ideal Versus Educational Reality

In no other institution of our society are the ideal and the reality so far apart as they are in education.

The ideal. The teacher is a sensitive monitor of the child's entire process of growth and development, entering into it in manifold ways, never to hamper, but always to encourage and guide development toward the fullest realization of the child's potentialities. There are other educational purposes (such as a nation's need for technically trained manpower), but no other ideal comes close to all-around acceptability in a free society, and with increasing prosperity and security we should expect that other educational purposes will drop out of competition with this ideal. Thus, when we speak of education in America, we speak of one ideal, shared by almost all educators, even though they differ as to how it should be pursued.

The reality. Two to three dozen captive children are placed in the charge of a teacher of only modest intellectual ability and little learning, where they spend approximately six hours a day engaged in activities that someone has decided are good for them. In the course of 12 years they acquire a certain amount of worthwhile skill and knowledge, but only on the rarest occasions, if at all, do they encounter anything even remotely resembling the kind of teacher-pupil interaction prescribed as ideal.

It Is Time to Question the Ideal

The ideal of humanistic education—"that education in which the primary function of the schools is to cultivate the 'independence' of each 'individual' and to develop each person to the fullest"—has been with us since ancient Greece.(1) Today, it is accepted as virtually beyond question. Educators occasionally accuse one another of holding conflicting ideals, but this is mere mudslinging. Every scheme for educational reform is an attempt, whether misguided or not, to bring reality closer to the humanistic ideal.

Perhaps the humanistic ideal cannot be questioned on ideal grounds, but it can be questioned on practical grounds. The question may be phrased as follows: Is it better to approximate the humanistic ideal as best we can, regardless of how far we fall short, or is it better to pursue some other ideal more in keeping with the limits imposed by reality?

This is a type of question that is all too seldom asked in the social sphere, although it is common in the industrial sphere, where, for instance, the ideal of producing a machine that will last forever is frequently supplanted by the ideal of producing a machine that will give maximum value per unit of cost. This type of question has recently begun to be asked in the social sphere by members of the "Third World," particularly by members of the Centro Intercultural de Documentacion. (2) As these social thinkers see it, underdeveloped countries have taken North American institutions and technologies as their "ideals" and have strived to approximate them as closely as possible, whereas, in view of the very limited economic resources of these countries, approximations to North American models are likely to be so remote as to be seriously dysfunctional and greatly inferior to institutions and technologies based on models suited to the economic and social realities of the countries involved. This line of reasoning is directly applicable to American education, which has the same problem of resources too limited for the model it tries to follow.

Talent as the Limiting Factor in Education

During the seventies it should become clear that lack of money is not the primary factor accounting for the great discrepancy between the educational ideal and reality. If we are unwise, we may learn this lesson through bitter experience. We may invest heavily in electronic and paraprofessional aides in order to free teachers to carry out humanistic education, only to find that they cannot do so any better than they do now. We may extend schooling down into earlier childhood, only to discover that we have spread the supply of competent teachers more thinly than before. We may increase teacher salaries only to find that the quality of teachers remains the same. We may increase the attractiveness of school buildings, equipment, and materials, only to find that students become increasingly disaffected. If, on the other hand, we are wise, we may foresee these results and channel our resources into other kinds of provisions for children that will yield greater social benefits, even though the benefits are not ones that we can properly call educational.

At the bottom of these dismal predictions is the simple premise that humanistic education calls for a supply of teacher talent that cannot possibly be met on the scale for universal education. Educational philosophers, when expounding their particular version of humanistic education, are always ready to admit that the talent required for teachers to bring it off is of a very high level. They seem to feel, however, that the talent can be produced by exhortation, and enormous amounts of educational ink go each year into resounding calls for greatness. If what is required ideally is something more than a Socrates, what is required for even a reasonable approximation is something not much less. Rousseau, who deserves first credit for reestablishing the humanistic ideal in the modern world, was less optimistic: "How can a child be well educated unless by one who is well educated himself ? Can this rare mortal be found? I do not know."(3)

The humanistic educator must be continually aware of the growing edge of the child's intellect and character. He must be exceedingly resourceful in seizing upon opportunities of the moment to turn them to educational account. To help the child learn, he must not only know what the child is to learn but know it so thoroughly that he can choose just the right question or demonstration or activity at just the right time. He cannot work from a prepared curriculum but must invent as he interacts with the child. He must at once be a good model and someone who does not force the child to be like himself or as he would like himself to be.

I could go on listing attributes, but let us try to jump from qualitative requirements to ones that can be quantified, realizing that much is lost in the process. It would stand to reason, I think, that a minimum requirement for such an educator—a bare minimum, indeed—would be an IQ of 115. Those who would object that some very clever people will earn IQ scores of less than this ought also to agree that their number will be offset by people of higher IQ who are not so clever. By this requirement we limit the potential teaching population to a sixth of the total work force. The other requirements, which have more to do with personality, are not so easily quantified, but we might reasonably judge that no more than half of the people who meet the intelligence requirements would possess the other personal characteristics needed to function adequately as humanistic educators. (4) This reduces the potential supply of educators to a twelfth of the labor force.

Projections of census totals for the labor force and the student population (including those in postsecondary education) into the seventies indicates that about two-thirds as many people will be in school as will be working. (5) Therefore, if everyone who had the minimum talent to teach did teach, we should have a teacher-pupil ratio of one-to-eight. This ratio would be scarcely sufficient to carry on the kind of teacher-pupil interaction required for personalistic education, which is ideally a one-to-one operation. But, of course, we cannot expect that all or even most of the people who could teach would teach, since the qualifications are ones that also fit an increasing number of other careers (including careers in education other than teaching).

Thus, if for no other reason, humanistic education must fail on grounds of a simple shortage of talent. This shortage, moreover, is one that cannot be remedied by any immediate action. Conceivably, better education would produce more people qualified to educate, but such improvement could only come about slowly over generations of students, and for all we know the trend may be downward rather than upward. Educational technology may relieve the teacher of many burdens—it might even be able to take over entirely the teaching of specific skills and knowledge—but what remains for the teacher is the very kind of creative person-to-person activity for which talent is most wanting.

Proposals for reform of the educational system, far from promising to alleviate the strain on talent resources, almost invariably call for more teachers of more exalted caliber. This is true of traditionalist schemes for a return to basic disciplines as it is of radical schemes for the abandonment of definite curricula. It could not be otherwise, for they are all efforts to bring practice closer to the ideal of humanistic education. We must apply to them Daniel P. Moynihan's dictum that "systems that require immense amounts of extraordinarily competent people to run them are not going to run." (6)

The Humanistic Ideal
Does More Harm Than Good

Thomas F. Green has claimed that, while educators almost universally claim to be pursuing humanistic education, what they do in reality is not concerned with developing individual potentialities but with training individuals to meet the needs of other institutions in the society. (7) It is no doubt true that what the public mainly expects of the schools is not the development of individual potentials but the teaching of socially useful skills—such as the three R's—and that the schools cannot avoid being responsive to this expectation. I believe it is incorrect, however, to infer from this that the commitment of educators to a humanistic ideology has no practical consequence.

In the first place, the humanistic commitment of educators has an effect—largely negative—on how they carry out their elementary training functions. In teaching reading and arithmetic, for instance, educators do not simply look for the most effective methods of achieving performance criteria. They tend to prefer, on ideological grounds, methods which seem to entail creativity, freedom of choice, discovery, challenges to thinking, democratic processes, and growth of self-knowledge. Moreover, they strive continually to win recognition for these values as more important than objective performance criteria.

In the second place, training in socially required skills does not begin to take up the entire school day. If schools restricted themselves to such training and attempted to do it as efficiently as possible, the school day might have to be only a third as long as it is now, and school costs could be lowered accordingly. Thus it is the addition of many other high-flown purposes, drawn from the humanistic ideal, that serves to justify the vast amount of time and money devoted to schooling and to motivate such costly proposals as year-round schooling and the extension of public education down into the early childhood years.

In the third place, educators are continually pressing for reforms that serve humanistic purposes in education. Nongrading, the open-plan school, the language experience approach, individualized instruction, and innovations of this sort are all reforms which would have the effect of shifting emphasis off training in elementary skills. Indeed, as these approaches come to be assimilated to common educational thinking, it becomes impossible to tell one from the other, because they all consist largely of reassertions of established tenets of humanistic education. And they all involve unrealistic requirements of teacher talent.

In the fourth place, humanistic values subtly infect the ways pupils and teachers are evaluated. Even if correctness and docility are still the attributes most consistently rewarded in students, there is a tendency for the less imaginative, insightful, or independent students to be regarded as failures; and such students are bound to get the message. Such students are put in a very agonizing position, since they are being condemned for failure to learn things that are not actually being taught. Teachers also tend to be evaluated and to evaluate themselves on how well they promote humanistic goals. Since these goals cannot be achieved, teachers are demoralized. Many of them are fine people and could be quite competent in training, but humanistic ideology often forces them to denigrate their own strengths.

This brings us to the last and most ignominious way in which humanistic ideology interacts with the training function of schools. It is that mechanisms of training are applied not only to the skill-learning purposes for which they are appropriate but also to other, humanistically-based purposes for which they are radically un-suited. The result is pseudotraining—ritualistic behavior that has the appearance of training but does not produce any of its desirable results. In social studies, science, and literature, teachers will often claim to be helping students to develop deep under-standing, thinking abilities, attitudes, interests, and values. Lacking any definite ways of promoting such development, howev-er, they fall back on memorization, lecture and exhortation, tasks that amount to no more than busy work, and endless practice. Even activities that are less mechanical, such as discussions, "proj-ects," experiments, themes, and field trips, are robbed of what in-trinsic merits they might have by efforts to turn them to educa-tional account. Discussions become mealy-mouthed, ill-timed, and pointless; projects become mere copy work; experiments turn into dull problems or the following of recipes; themes become exercises in grammar; and field trips become holidays.

Most of what is so tedious, unprofitable, phony, and "irrelevant" in schooling is done not in the name of training in basic skills but in the name of the highest-sounding humanistic objectives. Radical critics of education find this anomaly perverse, and seem to think that if only educators could get their values straight they would do better. But the anomaly is built into the very structure of mass ed-ucation. Most teachers cannot educate in the humanistic sense, and of those who can, few are able to do so even sporadically under the pupil loads they bear.

Current Movements
Away from Education

Under the impulse of humanistic ideology, many schools are moving away from the kind of pseudotraining I have described to a type of program in which the pupil is free much of the time to do what he wants. In practice, societal demands for training are usually still recognized, but only limited portions of the day are devoted to meeting them. Individual development is seen as some-thing that will occur pretty much by itself, and the teacher's main job is to refrain from obstructing it. One of the more recent trends is to get away from confining children to school at all, allowing them to pursue their interests in the community at large.

To the extent that development is truly left up to the child, this type of program amounts to the abandonment of humanistic educa-tion in favor of a more simplistic faith in nature. However, these types of programs carry, if anything, an even heavier burden of educational purpose than existing ones. As a result they are even more unrealistic and potentially harmful. The following are some of the disadvantages of this educational approach:

1) Expectations of personal growth in such areas as creativity and understanding are heightened, while the teacher is provided with even less that she can do to bring it about. This can induce a feeling of helplessness in teachers and failure in students.

2) The teacher is expected to monitor the growth process in subtle and unspecified ways, thus to function fully as a humanistic educator, which few teachers are talented enough to do.

3) Since the entire program is carried out under the auspices of the school system, it is continuously vulnerable to pressure from a public which expects something quite different from its schools.

4) The laissez-faire approach is frequently generalized to areas of skill training, where it will likely lead to a deterioration in achievement.

5) A concern to make activities educational is likely to lead to limiting the options open to children and to corruption of activities which they might otherwise enjoy.

6) Such programs are costly, not only because of the need to provide a greater variety of facilities and materials but also because more teachers are required to supervise children when they are all engaged in different activities. When educational programs are extended into the community, there are added costs from the greater demand for community facilities, while teacher costs increase even further. (8)

7) Providing an optimum environment is something that professional educators are not necessarily the best qualified people to do. An enormous variety of specialized talents are applicable, and there is no reason why the utilization of these talents should be centralized. Moreover, as a public institution the school system is barred from partisan, sectarian, or controversial activities that ought to be available to children under a truly open program.

Why Not Abandon the Effort
at Humanistic Education Altogether?

I have argued that current and proposed methods of carrying out humanistic education through the schools only make a mockery of it and that such education is impossible to achieve on a mass basis. Current movements away from education, however, suggest a logical next step consisting of the following changes:

1) Restrict the responsibility of the schools entirely to training in

well-defined, clearly teachable skills. This should require only about a third of the cost in money, personnel, and time that schooling costs now. What would be lost would be largely good riddance, and with exclusive concentration on training the schools could probably do a much more efficient and pleasing job of it than they do now.

2) Set children free the rest of the time to do what they want, but in doing so get them out from under the authority of the schools. Provide more economical forms of custodial care and guidance, as needed, and do it without educational intent.

3) Use the large amount of money thus saved to provide an enormously enriched supply of cultural resources for children, with which they can spend their new-found free time. These resources may reflect humanistic values to the fullest, but they should not carry any burden of educational intent, in the sense of trying to direct or improve upon the course of personal development. They should simply be resources and activities considered worthy in their own right.

4) Do not restrict children to these publicly sponsored activities. Maintain an open cultural market, in which proponents of diverse activities may compete to attract children to them.

This proposal has, I believe, all of the genuine advantages of the current movements toward freer, more humanistic education, while avoiding the seven faults noted above. In addition it has the potentiality of enriching the cultural life of our communities in ways by which all citizens would benefit—by increasing the supply of cultural resources, some of which would be of value to adults as well as children, and also by freeing young people to pursue activities through which they could contribute their talents to society.*

If humanistic education existed, it would be a shame to lose it; if it could exist we should try to achieve it. When I discuss with people this proposal to abandon pursuit of humanistic education, I am repeatedly met with personal anecdotes about the one teacher in a person's school career who changed his life, who opened up to him a vision of what he could become and started him on the road to becoming it. These single events are taken as sufficient to offset all the dross that filled most of their school days and to justify the continued, largely futile pursuit of the humanistic ideal of education. To this argument I would only reply that such rare encounters, which are indeed the essence of humanistic education, are more likely to occur in a system where children are free to seek their own contacts in the cultural world.

*I have in mind such possibilities as theater, music, and journalism produced by young people and youth participation in social action and scientific activities.

Suggestions for Governmental Action

1) There is already considerable support for research on the improvement of training in basic skills. This should continue and be made freer than it is now of ideological obstructions. There is considerable pressure from educational ideologues to suppress training research that does not conform sufficiently to humanistic educational expectations. It should be recognized that such expectations are irrelevant to the training function of schools. There should be special encouragement of research which seeks to extend the range of what is actually teachable. Thinking skills, for instance, are not now teachable to any significant extent, but some of them might be.

2) Support programs of teacher training that develop training skills. Most teachers receive no relevant training of any kind; they only learn *about* teaching and *about* children. If schools are to train, teachers must learn how to do it, and this is something that ordinary teachers could learn.

3) Support the development of new kinds of cultural opportunities for children to take the place of schooling. This type of development should not be done predominantly by educators, and supervision of it should probably not be in the hands of the Office of Education, since it is not an educational undertaking. Various agencies concerned with arts, sciences, recreation, and communications should be empowered to support such work on the part of creative people from all walks of life.

4) Model programs along the lines set forth in the preceding section should be instituted to work out the numerous problems and to explore the numerous possibilities associated with the disbanding of a century-old institution and the creation of a new way of serving the nation's youth.

From *Needs of Elementary and Secondary Education for the Seventies. A Compendium of Policy Papers.* Compiled by the General Subcommittee on Education of the House of Representatives Committee on Education and Labor, Ninety-First Congress, Washington, D.C.: U.S. Government Printing Office, March, 1970, pp. 29-36.

Notes

1. The definition is from Thomas F. Green, "Schools and Communities: A Look Forward," *Harvard Educational Review, 39* (Spring 1969), 235. The somewhat more descriptive but less familiar term "personalist education" is used by H. I. Marrou in his *History of Education in Antiquity* (New York: Sheed and Ward, 1956).
2. See Ivan Illich, "Outwitting the 'Developed' Countries," *New York Review of Books, 13* (November 6, 1969), 20-24.
3. William Boyd, *The Emile of Jean Jacques Rosseau, 3* (New York: Bureau of Publications, Teachers College, Columbia University, 1962), p. 19.

4. This estimate is probably too generous. Generally too little is known to permit the meaningful setting of minimum scores on personality tests, as was done with IQ. However, the Myers-Briggs Type Indicator (Isabell Briggs Myers. *Manuel: The Myers-Briggs Type Indicator*, Princeton, New Jersey: Educational Testing Service, 1962), based on Jungian theory, provides a classification of people into types that is relevant to this issue. It seems reasonable that humanistic educators should be "intuitive" rather than "sense-perceptive" (fact-bound) types and that they should be "perceiving" (open to many possibilities) rather than "judging" types. A classification of nearly 4,000 students in highly-selective liberal arts colleges (who could therefore be presumed to meet the intelligence requirement) showed that only about a third of them qualify in both categories (*ibid*, p. 45).

5. U.S. Bureau of the Census, *Statistical Abstract of the United States: 1969* (Washington, D.C.: U.S. Government Printing Office, 1969), pp. 103 and 212.

6. Quoted in *The Futurist, 3* (August, 1969), 100.

7. Green, pp. 235-236.

8. This is true, at least, of the first major experiment along these lines, the Parkway Project in Philadelphia. See D. Cox, "Learning on the Road: Parkway Project, Philadelphia," *Saturday Review, 52* (May 17, 1969), 71.

III

Selection from *The New Reformation: Notes of a Neolithic Conservative*

Paul Goodman

Argument for Incidental Education

It is arguable that the chief problem in the coming generation will be survival—whether surviving nuclear blasts, genocide, ecological disaster, or mass starvation and endless wars. But if so, this would be the present task of pedagogy. There already exist wilderness schools for self-reliance, and it has been proposed that guerrilla warfare be the curriculum in Harlem schools. The delicately interlocking technologies and overgrown cities are indeed terribly vulnerable, and the breakdown could be pretty fatal.

. . . I do not believe in this apocalyptic future of the breakdown of civilization. Rather, my own "Reformation" thinking about education is as follows:

1) Incidental education, taking part in the ongoing activities of society, must again be made the chief means of learning and teaching.

2) Most high schools should be eliminated, with other kinds of youth communities taking over their sociable functions.

3) College training should generally follow, rather than precede, entry into the professions.

4) The chief occupation of educators should be to see to it that the activities of society provide incidental education, rather than exploitation or neglect. If necessary, we must invent new useful activities that offer educational opportunities.

5) The purpose of elementary pedagogy, through age twelve, should be to delay socialization, to protect children's free growth, since our families and community both pressure them too much and do not attend to them enough. Modern times pollute and waste natural human resources, the growing children, just as they do the land, air, and water. What else could one expect?

Incidental Education versus Schooling

Let me review the arguments for this program. We must drastically cut back formal schooling because the present extended tutelage is against nature and arrests growth. . . . Schooling isolates the young from the older generation and alienates them.

As it is, to be sure, the actual activities of American society either exclude the young or exploit them or corrupt them. Here is the task for educators. We must make the rules of licensing and hiring realistic to the actual work and get rid of mandarin requirements. We must design apprenticeships that are not exploitative. Society desperately needs much work that is not now done, both intellectual and manual, in urban renewal, rural reconstruction, ecology, communications, and the arts, and all these could make use of young people. Many activities, like community development and Vocations for Social Change, can be well organized by young people themselves. Little think tanks like the Oceanic Institute at Makapuu Point or the Institute for Policy Studies in Washington, which are not fussy about diplomas, have provided excellent training for the young. There is need for many thousands of centers of design and research, and local newspapers, radio stations, and theaters.

Our aim should be to multiply the paths of growing up, instead of narrowing the one existing school path. There must be opportunity to start again after false starts, to cross over, take a moratorium, travel, work on one's own. To insure freedom of option, so that the young can maintain and express their critical attitude, all adolescents should be guaranteed a living. (The present cost of high school and the first years of college is enough to pay for this.)

Of course, the advantage of making education less academic has occurred to school people too. There are a myriad of programs to open the schools to the world—on the one hand by importing outside professionals, artists in residence, gurus, mothers, and dropouts as teachers' aides; and on the other hand by exporting academic credit for work-study, community action, writing novels, service in mental hospitals, junior year abroad, and other kinds of released time. Naturally I am enthusiastic about these developments. I only want the school people to go the small further step of abolishing the present school establishment, instead of using these means to aggrandize it.

There is some talk in the United States (and some actual practice in China and Cuba) about adolescent years being devoted to public service. This is good if the service is not compulsory and regimenting. It is one good option.

It is possible for every education to be tailor-made according to each youth's developing interest and choice. Youthful choices along the way will be very often ill-conceived and wasteful, but they will express desire and immediately meet reality, and therefore they should converge on right vocation more quickly than by any other course. Vocation is what one is good at and can do, what uses a reasonable amount of one's powers and gives one a useful occupation in a community that is one's own. The right use of choice by the majority of people would make a stable society far more efficient than our own. Some, perhaps many, have peculiar excellences that no social planning can anticipate, but these are more likely to find their own way further if they have had entry into a field where they are competent and are accepted. It was Goethe's wise advice to a young man not to try to do what he wished, which would almost certainly prove to be deceptive, but to get engaged in life by doing something he was competent at and then to seize opportunities that might arise; these would lead to what he more deeply wanted and what he ought to do.

Those with academic talents can choose academic schools, and such schools are better off unencumbered by the sullen uninterested bodies of the others. But the main use of academic teaching is for those already busy in sciences and professions who need academic courses along the way. (Cooper Union in New York City used to fulfill this function very well.) And in this context of real motivation, there can finally be the proper use of new pedagogic technology as a means of learning at one's own time and pace, whereas at present this technology makes the school experience still more rigid and impersonal.

Inevitably, in this setup, employers would themselves provide ancillary academic training, especially if they had to pay for it anyway, instead of using parents' and taxpayers' money. In my opinion, this ancillary, rather than prior schooling, would do more than any other single thing to give black, rural, and other "culturally deprived" youths a fairer entry and chance for advancement, since what is to be learned ancillary to the job is objective and functional and does not depend on the abstract school style. On the job, as we have seen, there is no correlation between competence and years of prior schooling.

But with schooling on the job, another problem emerges. Educationally, schooling on the job is usually superior; it has reality and motivation. But the political and moral consequences of such a system are ambiguous. The difficulty is not, as is usually the objection, that such training is narrow, for "comprehensive" schooling does not produce "well-rounded" people either; and if a job does not have humane bearings, perhaps it is not worth doing at all. But on-the-job training does put the young under the control of the employer, whether private, corporate, or state. At present in the United States, a young person is hired on the basis of actual credentials; these have cost him wasted years and they rarely signify any actual skill, but he brings them as his own, he has gotten them elsewhere. This is alienating to him as a person, but it does give him a measure of free-market power; he has something to contract with. If he is to be schooled on the job, however, he must be hired for his promise and attended to as a person. This is less alienating, but it can lead to company paternalism, like Japanese capitalism or like Fidel Castro's Marxist vision of farm- and factory-based schools. On the other hand, if the young have a secure living, have options, and can organize and criticize, on-the-job education is the quickest way to workers' management which, in my opinion, is the only effective industrial democracy. . . .

To provide a protective and life-nourishing environment for children up through twelve, Summerhill is an adequate model and can easily be adapted to urban conditions, especially if we include houses of refuge for children to resort to, when necessary, to escape parental and neighborhood tyranny or terror. . . . The goal of elementary education should be a very modest one: it is for a small child, under his own steam, not on a leash, to be able to poke interestedly into whatever goes on and to be able, by observation, questions, and practical imitation, to get something out of it on his own terms. In our society this happens pretty well at home up to age four, but after that it becomes forbiddingly difficult.

Thoughts on Teaching to Read

A big obstacle to children's learning to read is the school setting in which they have to pick it up. For any learning to be skillful and lasting, it must be or become second nature, self-motivated; and for this, schooling is too impersonal, standardized, and scheduled. If we tried to teach infants to speak by academic methods in an environment like school, my guess is that many would fail and most would stammer.

The analogy between learning to speak and learning to read is not exact, but it is instructive to pursue it, since, in principle, speaking should be much harder to pick up. As many philosophers have pointed out, learning to speak is a stupendous intellectual achievement, involving the use of signs, acquiring a vocabulary, and mastering an extraordinary kind of algebra—syntax, with almost infinite variables in a large number of sentence forms. Yet almost all succeed, equally well, no matter what their class or culture, though they learn a different vocabulary and syntax depending on their class or culture. Every child picks up a dialect, "correct" or "incorrect," adequate to express the thoughts and needs of his milieu.

We do not know, scientifically, how children learn to speak, but we can describe some of the indispensable conditions:

1) The child is constantly exposed to speech related to interesting behavior in which he often shares. ("Now, where's your little coat? We're going to the supermarket. It's cold out today.")
2) The speakers are persons important to the child, and they often single him out to speak to or about him.
3) The child plays with the sounds, tries them out, freely imitates what he hears, approximates it without interference or correction. When he succeeds, he is rewarded by attention and other useful results.
4) Later, the child consolidates by his own will what he has learned. He promotes himself or graduates, so to speak, as an accomplished speaker by leaving his grownup first teachers. From age three to five he acquires style, accent, and fluency by speaking with his peers, adopting their uniform, but also asserting his own tone. He speaks peer speech more than parent speech, but he is uniquely recognizable as speaking in his own voice and way.

We can infer the "naturalness" or normalcy of this process from the derangements that occur when conditions are amiss. If the parents are mute, the infant does not learn to speak. If there is demand and expectation, a common result is stuttering. If there is emotional disturbance in other functions of growing up, like being weaned, there may be certain speech defects, like lisping. If the parents instill a middle-class self-consciousness (guiltiness), the syntax abounds in the use of "I" and indirect discourse. In a culture of poverty, there are few complex sentences, and physical nudging and hitting occur instead of growth of vocabulary. (Wordsworth observed the cultural conditions of good and bad speech perhaps better than anybody else.)

Now suppose, by contrast, that we tried to teach speaking by academic methods in a school setting:

1) Speaking would be a curricular subject abstracted from the web of activity and reserved for special hours punctuated by bells. It might even be forbidden for nonprofessionals to talk to the infants, since this would interfere with the proper method.

2) Speaking would be a tool subject rather than a way of being in the world.

3) It would not spring from the child's needs in immediate situations but would be taught according to the teacher's idea of his future advantage, perhaps aiming at his getting a job sixteen years later or being admitted to an elite college.

4) Along the way, therefore, the child would have to be "motivated," the exercises would have to be "fun." In order to make up for the skimpiness of experience in the classroom, it might be wise to provide audio-visual aids.

5) The lessons would be arranged in a graded series from simple to complex. It would be generally held that learning monosyllables precedes polysyllables. Some would hold that words precede sentences and must be mastered first; others would hold that sentences precede words. Perhaps the Head Start curriculum would be devoted to the phonemes, in order to assure later articulateness, or the first hour should specialize in nouns; the second, in verbs. The second semester could put these together.

6) The teacher's relation to the infant would be further depersonalized by the need to speak or listen to only what suits two dozen other children as well.

7) Being continually called on, corrected, tested, and evaluated to meet a standard in a group, some children would become stutterers. Others would devise a phony system of apparently speaking in order to get by—the speech would mean nothing. Others would balk at being processed and would purposely become stupid. Some of these would get remedial courses. Others would play hooky and go to special infant jails.

8) Since there is a predetermined range of what can be spoken and how it must be spoken—decided ultimately in the state capital or according to the guidelines of the National Science Foundation— everybody's speech would be standard and unlike any native dialect. (You can hear this exotic product among principals in the New York City school system.) Expression of the child's own experience or feeling would be discouraged by various kinds of negative conditioning.

Evaluating the Present System of Reading

These eight disastrous conceptions are not an unfair caricature of how we teach reading. Reading is treated as abstract, instrumental, irrelevant to actual needs, extrinsically motivated, impersonal, standarized, not expressive of truth or art. The teaching often produces awkwardness, faking, and balking. Let me also make a few further points specific to reading.

1) Omitting their prima facie functions as reminders, signs, com-

munication with absent persons, self-expression, and studied formulation, writing and reading are astoundingly divorced from the speaking which is their matrix. Teachers of freshman English in colleges discover that, for the majority of the students, writing and reading have no intrinsic relation to saying and hearing. Especially writing—"compositions"—is a tortured song and dance that has no connection with saying something or having something to say. Speech, too, has been ossified. It is really necessary to unteach everything and go back to psychosomatic exercises in babbling, free association, and saying and writing dirty words. And young people consider it quite plausible when Marshall McLuhan and others say that writing and reading will pass away, as if mankind were going to give up talking as the primary way of communicating, expressing themselves, and being in the world. But people are going to go on talking and, hopefully, writers will continue to renew speech.

2) Most people who have learned to read and write fluently have done so on their own with their own material, whether library books, newspapers, comic books, or street signs. They may, or may not, have picked up the ABC's in school, but they acquired skill and preserved what they had learned on their own. This self-learning is important, for it is not at the mechanical level of ABC's that reading retardation drastically occurs, but in the subsequent years when the good readers are going it alone and the others are either signing off and forgetting or settling for a vestigial skill that makes it impossible for them ever to read an authentic book.

3) According to some neurophysiologists, given the exposure to written code in modern urban and suburban conditions, any emotionally normal child in middle-class surroundings will spontaneously learn to read by age nine, just as he learned to speak by age three. It is impossible for him not to pick up the code unless he is systematically interrupted and discouraged, for instance by tring to teach him in school.

Of course, children of the culture of poverty do not have the ordinary middle-class need for literacy and the premium put on it, and they are less exposed to it among their parents and peers. Thus for these children there is a use for the right kind of schooling.

4) Against my argument here, it seems that in all modern countries school methods, lessons, copying, and textbooks, have been used successfully to teach children to read. But this evidence is deceptive. High competence was expected of very few, e.g., in 1900 in the United States only 6 percent graduated from high school. Little effort was made with children of the working class and none at all with those from the culture of

poverty. It is inherently unlikely that the same procedures could work with the present change of scale and population. Where a dramatic effort has been made to teach adults to read, en masse, as in Cuba, the method has been informal—"each one teach one."

5) Also, the experience of freshman English shows that achieving a test score adequate for college entrance does not prove much. John Holt has described the subtle devices that are learned in order to get by in a good middle-class high school; for this is the real life problem, not reading and writing. The case is analogous to the large group among Puerto Rican children in New York who apparently speak English well but who in fact cannot say anything that they need or mean, such as "Pass the salt" or "My friend is in jail." They are just putting on a performance. But unless reading serves for truth and art, why bother? We have seen that it's not much use on most jobs, except for getting hired. Radio, television, and movies give other satisfactions more easily.

The Mini-School Proposal

Is it possible and feasible to teach reading somewhat in the way children learn to speak: by intrinsic interest, with personal attention, and in an environment less isolated from life than our schools? Pedagogically and economically, it is possible. The following was roughly the model for the First Street School on the Lower East Side in New York City, and the cost there was approximate to that in the New York public schools, $900 per child at that time. Politically, however, such a solution is unlikely, since it threatens both vested interests and popular prejudices.

For ages six to eleven I propose a system of tiny schools, radically decentralized. By decentralization I here do not mean "community control"—which is a political good that I have been urging for twenty years—but decentralization to the level of actual operation: a mini-school would have about twenty-eight children and four teachers, and each tiny school would be largely administered by its own staff and parents with considerable say also by the children, as in Summerhill.

The four teachers are

1) A teacher licensed and salaried as in the present system. Since the present average class size is twenty-eight, these are available.

2) A graduating college senior from one of the local colleges, perhaps embarking on graduate study. Salary, $2000. There is no lack of candidates, young people who want to do something useful and interesting in a free setting.

3) A literate housewife and mother, who can also prepare lunch. Salary, $4000. Again there is no lack of candidates.
4) A literate, willing, and intelligent high school graduate or dropout. Salary, $2000. No lack of candidates.

The staff in New York City should be black, white, and Puerto Rican. And it is the case, demonstrated by the First Street School, that in a small setup with children getting individual attention, it is easy to have mixed classes. Middle-class parents, at least in New York, do not withdraw when they do not fear that their children will be swamped and retarded. Black parents can be persuaded that the setup is useful for the children. Spanish-speaking children will come if their friends come.

For its setting, the mini-school would occupy two, three, or four rooms in existing school buildings or church basements and settlement houses otherwise empty during school hours, rooms set aside in housing built by public funds, and rented storefronts. The layout is fairly indifferent, since a major part of activity would occur outside the place. The place should be able to be transformed into a clubhouse, decorated and equipped according to the group's own decision. It is good for the school to be on the street where the children live so that they can come and go at will; but there is also an advantage in locating in racial and ethnic border areas to increase the chance of intermixture. For purposes of assembly, health services, and some games, ten tiny schools can unite and use present public school facilities.

The cost saving would be the almost total elimination of top-down administration and the kind of special services that are required because of size and rigidity. The chief uses of central administration would be funding, licensing, finding sites, and making some inspection. There would be no principals and assistants, secretaries and assistants. Curriculum, texts, equipment are to be decided as needed—and despite the present putative economies of scale, they would be cheaper, since less is pointless or wasted—and the secondhand and hand-me-down are quite adequate. Record keeping would be at a minimum. There is no need for truant officers when a teacher-and-six call at the absentee's home and inquire. There is little need for remedial personnel, since the staff and parents are always in contact and the whole enterprise can be regarded as remedial. Studies of large top-down directed enterprises, in which persons are the main cost, show that the total cost is invariably at least 300 percent above the cost of the function—in this case the interaction of teachers, children, and parents. We here would put this 300 percent saving into increasing the number of grownups and diversifying the possibilities of experience. Finally in the conditions of big city real estate, there is great advantage in fitting schools into available niches rather than building $4 million school buildings.

This model permits natural learning of reading. There can be exposure to activities of the city. A teacher-and-seven can spend most of the time on the streets, in a playground, visiting business offices, watching television, at a museum, chatting with the corner druggist, riding the buses and subways, visiting rich and poor homes. Such experiences are saturated with speaking, reading and writing. For instance, a group might choose to spend several weeks at the Museum of Natural History relabeling the exhibits for their own level of comprehension, and the curator would be well advised to allot them a couple of hundred dollars to do it.

Each child can be addressed according to his own style and interests in choice of reading matter. Given so many contexts, a teacher can easily strike when the iron is hot, whether reading the destination of a bus or the label on a can of soup. If some children catch on quickly and forge ahead on their own, the teacher need not waste their time and can concentrate on the others. The setting does not prejudge as to formal or informal techniques, phonics, Montessori, rote drill, Moore's typewriter, labeling the furniture, or any other method.

As a writer, I like Sylvia Ashton-Warner's method of teaching little Maoris to read. Each day she tried to catch the most passionate concern of each child as he came in and to give him a card with that key word—usually the words were those of fear, anger, hunger, loneliness, sexual desire. Soon each child had a large, ineradicable, and very peculiar reading list, not at all like *Dick and Jane*. He would then easily progress to reading and writing anything. From the beginning in this method, reading and writing are gut-meaningful; they express truth and feeling. . . .

For the first five school years there is no merit in the standard curriculum. To repeat Dewey's maxim, for a small child everything in the environment is educative if he attends to it with guidance. In any case, normal children can learn the standard eight years' curriculum in about four months at age twelve.

And there is little merit for this age in the usual teacher training. Any literate and well-intentioned grownup or late teen-ager knows enough to teach a small child many things. . . .

The chief criterion for selecting a staff is the one I have mentioned: liking children and being willing to be attentive to them. But given this setting, which they can more or less run as they will, many young people would go into teaching and continue, whereas in the New York system the annual turnover approaches 20 percent after years of wasted training and an elaborate routine of testing and hiring.

From *New Reformation*, by Paul Goodman. Copyright © 1970 by Paul Goodman. Reprinted by permission of Random House, Inc.

IV

Education
without School:
How It Can Be Done

Ivan Illich

A New Style
of Educational Relationship

In a previous article(1) I discussed what is becoming a common complaint about schools—one that is reflected, for example, in the recent report of the Carnegie Commission: In school registered students submit to certified teachers in order to obtain certificates of their own; both are frustrated and both blame insufficient resources—money, time, or buildings—for their mutual frustration.

Such criticism leads many people to ask whether it is possible to conceive of a different style of learning. The same people, paradoxically, when pressed to specify how they acquired what they know and value, will readily admit that they learned it more often outside than inside school. Their knowledge of facts, their understanding of life and work came to them from friendship or love, while viewing TV or while reading, from examples of peers or the challenge of a street encounter. Or they may have learned what they know through the apprenticeship ritual for admission to a street gang or the initiation to a hospital, newspaper city room, plumber's shop, or insurance office. The alternative to dependence on schools is not the use of public resources for some new device which *makes* people learn, rather it is the creation of a new style of educational relationship between man and his environment. To foster this style, attitudes toward growing up, the tools available for learning, and the quality and structure of daily life will have to change concurrently.

Attitudes are already changing. The proud dependence on school is gone. Consumer resistance is increasing in the knowledge industry. Many teachers and pupils, taxpayers and employers, economists and policemen would prefer not to depend any longer on schools. What prevents their frustration from shaping new institutions is a lack not only of imagination but frequently also one of appropriate language and of enlightened self-interest. They cannot visualize either a deschooled society or educational institutions in a society which disestablishes school.

In this essay, I intend to show that the *inverse of school* is possible: that we can depend on self-motivated learning instead of employing teachers to bribe or compel the student to find time and the will to learn; that we can provide the learner with new links to the world instead of continuing to funnel all educational programs through the teacher. I shall discuss some of the general characteristics which distinguish *schooling* from *learning* and outline four major categories of educational institutions which should appeal not only to many individuals but also to many existing interest groups.

An Objection: Who Can Be Served by Bridges to Nowhere?

We are used to considering schools as a variable, dependent on the political and economic structure. If we can change the style of political leadership, or promote the interests of one class or another, or switch from private to public ownership of the means of production, we assume the school system will change as well. The educational institutions I will propose, however, are meant to serve a society which does not now exist, although the current frustration with schools is itself potentially a major force to set in motion change toward new social arrangements. An obvious objection has been raised to this approach: Why channel energy to build bridges to nowhere, instead of marshaling it first to change not the schools but the political and economic system?

This objection, however, underestimates the repressive political and economic nature of the school system itself, as well as the political potential inherent in a new educational style. In a basic sense, schools have ceased to be dependent on the ideology professed by a government or the organization of its market. Even the Chinese feel they must adopt the basic international structure of schooling in order to become a world power and a nation state. Control of society is reserved everywhere to those who have consumed at least four units of four years, each unit consisting of 500 to 1000 hours in the classroom.

School, as I suggested in my previous article, is the major component of the system of consumer production which is becoming more complex and specialized and bureaucratized. Schooling is necessary to produce the habits and expectations of the managed consumer society. Inevitably it produces institutional dependence and ranking in spite of any effort by the teacher to teach the contrary. It is an illusion that schools are only a dependent variable—an illusion which, moreover, provides them, the reproductive organs of a consumer society, with their immunity.

Even the piecemeal creation of new educational agencies which are the inverse of school would therefore be an attack on the most sensitive link of a pervasive phenomenon, which is organized by the state in all countries. A political program which does not explicitly recognize the need for deschooling is not revolutionary; it is demagoguery calling for more of the same. Any major political program of the seventies should be evaluated by this measure: How clearly does it state the need for deschooling, and how clearly does it provide guidelines for the educational quality of the society for which it aims?

The struggle against domination by the world market and big power politics might be beyond some poor communities or countries, but this weakness is an added reason for emphasizing the importance of liberating each society through a reversal of its educational structure, a change which is not beyond any society's means.

General Characteristics of New Formal Educational Institutions

A good educational system should have three purposes: it should provide all who want to learn with access to available resources at any time in their lives; empower all who want to share what they know to find those who want to learn it from them; and, finally, furnish all who want to present an issue to the public with the opportunity to make their challenge known. Such a system would require the application of constitutional guarantees to education. Learners should not be enforced to submit to an obligatory curriculum or to discrimination based on whether they possess a certificate or a diploma. Nor should the public be forced to support—

through a regressive taxation—a huge professional apparatus of educators and buildings which in fact restricts the public's chances for learning to the services the profession is willing to put on the market. It should use modern technology to make free speech, free assembly, and a free press truly universal and, therefore, fully educational.

Schools are designed on the assumption that there is a secret to everything in life, that the quality of life depends on knowing that secret, that secrets can be known only in orderly successions, and that only teachers can properly reveal these secrets. An individual with a schooled mind conceives of the world as a pyramid of classified packages accessible only to those who carry the proper tags. New educational institutions would break apart this pyramid. Their purpose must be to facilitate access for the learner: to allow him to look into the windows of the control room or the parliament, if he cannot get in the door. Moreover, such new institutions should be channels to which the learner would have access without credentials or pedigree—public spaces in which peers and elders outside his immediate horizon now become available.

I believe that no more than four—possibly even three—distinct "channels" or learning exchanges could contain all the resources needed for real learning. The child grows up in a world of things, surrounded by people who serve as models for skills and values. He finds peers who challenge him to argue, to compete, to cooperate, and to understand; and if the child is lucky, he is exposed to confrontation or criticism by an experienced elder who really cares. Things, models, peers, and elders are four resources—each of which requires a different type of arrangement to ensure that everybody has ample access to them.

I will use the word "network" to designate specific ways to provide access to each of four sets of resources. The word is often used, unfortunately, to designate the channels reserved to material selected by others for indoctrination, instruction, and entertainment. But it can also be used for the telephone or the postal service, which are primarily accessible to individuals who want to send messages to one another. What are needed are new networks, readily available to the public and designed to spread equal opportunity for learning and teaching.

To give an example: The same level of technology is used in TV and in tape recorders. All Latin American countries now have introduced TV; in Bolivia the government has financed a TV station, which was built six years ago, and there are no more than 7,000 TV sets for four million citizens. The money now tied up in TV installations throughout Latin America could have provided every fifth adult with a tape recorder. In addition, the money would have sufficed to provide an almost unlimited library of prerecorded tapes, with outlets even in remote villages, as well as an ample supply of empty tapes.

This network of tape recorders, of course, would be radically different from the present network of TV. It would provide opportunity for free expression: literate and illiterate alike could record, preserve, disseminate, and repeat their opinions. The present investment in TV instead provides bureaucrats, whether politicians or educators, with the power to sprinkle the continent with institutionally produced programs which they—or their sponsors—decide are good for or in demand by the people. Technology is available to develop either independence and learning or bureaucracy and preaching.

Four Networks

The planning of new educational institutions ought not to begin with the administrative goals of a principal or president, or with the teaching goals of a professional educator, or with the learning goals of any hypothetical class of people. It must not start with the question, "What should someone learn?" but with the question, "What kinds of things and people might learners want to be in contact with in order to learn?"

Someone who wants to learn knows that he needs both information and critical response to its use from somebody else. Information can be stored in things and in persons. In a good educational system, access to things ought to be available at the sole bidding of the learner, while access to informants requires, in addition, others' consent. Criticism can also come from two directions: from peers or from elders, that is, from fellow learners whose immediate interests match his own or from those who will grant him a share in their superior experience. Peers can be colleagues with whom to raise a question, companions for playful and enjoyable (or arduous) reading or walking, challengers at any type of game. Elders can be consultants on which skill to learn, which method to use, what company to seek at a given moment. They can be guides to the right questions to be raised among peers and to the deficiency of answers they arrive at.

Educational resources are usually labeled according to educators' curricular goals. I propose to do the contrary, to label four different approaches which enable the student to gain access to any educational resource which may help him to define and achieve his own goals:

1) Reference Services to Educational Objects—which facilitate access to things or processes used for formal learning. Some of these things can be reserved for this purpose, stored in

libraries, rental agencies, laboratories, and showrooms like museums and theaters; others can be in daily use in factories, in airports, or on farms but made available to students as apprentices or on off-hours.

2) Skill Exchanges—which permit persons to list their skills, the conditions under which they are willing to serve as models for others who want to learn these skills, and the addresses at which they can be reached.

3) Peer Matching—a communication network which permits persons to describe the learning activity in which they wish to engage in the hope of finding a partner for the inquiry.

4) Reference Services to Educators-at-large—who can be listed in a directory giving the addresses and self-descriptions of professionals, paraprofessionals, and free-lancers, along with conditions of access to their services. Such educators, as we will see, could be chosen by polling or consulting their former clients.

Reference Services to Educational Objects

Things are basic resources for learning. The quality of the environment and the relationship of a person to it will determine how much he learns incidentally. Formal learning requires special access to ordinary things, on the one hand, or, on the other, easy and dependable access to special things made for educational purposes. An example of the former is the special right to operate or dismantle a machine in a garage. An example of the latter is the general right to use an abacus, a computer, a book, a botanical garden, or a machine withdrawn from production and placed at the full disposal of students.

At present, attention is focused on the disparity between rich and poor children in their access to things and in the manner in which they can learn from them. OEO and other agencies, following this approach, concentrate on equalizing chances by trying to provide more educational equipment for the poor. A more radical point of departure would be to recognize that in the city rich and poor alike are artificially kept away from most of the things that surround them. Children born into the age of plastics and efficiency experts must penetrate two barriers which obstruct their understanding: one built into things and the other around institutions. Industrial design creates a world of things that resist insight into their nature, and schools shut the learner out of the world of things in their meaningful setting.

After a short visit to New York, a woman from a Mexican village told me she was impressed by the fact that stores sold "only wares heavily made up with cosmetics." I understood her to mean that industrial products "speak" to their customers about their allurements and not about their nature. Industry has surrounded people with artifacts whose inner workings only specialists are allowed to understand. The nonspecialist is discouraged from figuring out what makes a watch tick, or a telephone ring, or an electric typewriter work by being warned that it will break if he tries. He can be told what makes a transistor radio work but he cannot find out for himself. This type of design tends to reinforce a noninventive society in which the experts find it progressively easier to hide behind their expertise and beyond evaluation.

The man-made environment has become as inscrutable as nature is for the primitive. At the same time, educational materials have been monopolized by school. Simple educational objects have been expensively packaged by the knowledge industry. They have become specialized tools for professional educators, and their cost has been inflated by forcing them to stimulate either environments or teachers.

The teacher is jealous of the textbook he defines as his professional implement. The student may come to hate the lab because he associates it with school work. The administrator rationalizes his protective attitude toward the library as a defense of costly public equipment against those who would play with it rather than learn. In this atmosphere, the student too often uses the map, the lab, the encyclopedia, or the microscope at the rare moments when the curriculum tells him to do so. Even the great classics become part of "sophomore year" instead of marking a new turn in a person's life. School removes things from everyday use by labeling them educational tools.

If we are to deschool, both tendencies must be reversed. The general physical environment must be made accessible, and those physical learning resources which have been reduced to teaching instruments must become generally available for self-directed learning. Using things merely as part of a curriculum can have an even worse effect than just removing them: it can corrupt the attitudes of pupils.

Games are a case in point. I do not mean the "games" of the physical education department (such as football and basketball), which the schools use to raise income and prestige and in which they have made a substantial capital investment. As the athletes themselves are well aware, these enterprises, which take the form of warlike tournaments, have undermined the playfulness of sports and are used to reinforce the competitive nature of schools. Rather I have in mind the educational games which can provide a unique way to penetrate formal systems. Set-theory, linguistics, propositional logic, geometry, physics, and even chemistry reveal themselves with little effort to certain persons who play these games. A friend of mine went to a Mexican market with a game called "Wff 'n Proof," which consists of some dice on which twelve logical symbols are imprinted. He showed children which two or three combinations constituted a well-formed sentence, and inductively, within the first hour, some onlookers also grasped the principle. Within a few hours of playfully conducting formal logical proofs, some children are capable of introducing others to the fundamental proofs of propositional logic. The others just walk away.

In fact, for some children such games are a special form of liberating education, since they heighten their awareness of the fact that formal systems are built on changeable axioms and that conceptual operations have a game-like nature. They are also simple, cheap, and—to a large extent—can be organized by the players themselves. Used outside the curriculum, such games provide an opportunity for identifying and developing unusual talent, while the school psychologist will often identify those who have such talent as in danger of becoming antisocial, sick, or unbalanced. Within school, when used in the form of tournaments, games are not only removed from the sphere of leisure, they often become tools used to translate playfulness into competition, a lack of abstract reasoning into a sign of inferiority. An exercise which is liberating for some character types becomes a strait jacket for others.

The control of school over educational equipment has still another effect. It increases enormously the cost of such cheap materials. Once their use is restricted to scheduled hours, professionals are paid to supervise their acquisition, storage, and use. Then students vent their anger against the school on the equipment, which must be purchased once again.

Paralleling the untouchability of teaching tools is the impenetrability of modern junk. In the thirties, any self-respecting boy knew how to repair an automobile, but now car makers multiply wires and withhold manuals from everyone except specialized mechanics. In a former era, an old radio contained enough coils and condensers to build a transmitter that would make all the neighborhood radios scream in feedback. Transistor radios are more portable, but nobody dares to take them apart. To change this in the highly industrialized countries will be immensely difficult; but at least in the Third World, we must insist on built-in educational qualities.

To illustrate my point, let me present a model: By spending $10 million it would be possible to connect 40,000 hamlets in a country like Peru with a spiderweb of six-foot-wide trails and maintain these, and, in addition, provide the country with 200,000 three-wheeled mechanical donkeys—five on the average for each hamlet. Few poor countries of this size spend less than this yearly on cars and roads, both of which are now mainly restricted to the rich and their employees while poor people remain trapped in their villages. Each of these simple but durable little vehicles would cost $125—half of which would pay for transmission and a six horsepower motor. A "donkey" could make 20 mph, and it can carry loads of 850 pounds (that is, most things besides trunks and steel beams, which are ordinarily moved).

The political appeal of such a transportation system to a peasantry is obvious. Equally obvious is the reason why those who hold power—and thereby automatically have a car—are not interested in spending money on trails and in clogging roads with engine-driven donkeys. The universal donkey could work only if a country's leaders were willing to impose a national speed limit of, say, 25 mph and adapt its public institutions to this. The model could not work if conceived only as a stopgap.

This is not the place to elaborate on the political, social, economic, financial, and technical feasibility of this model.(2) I only wish to indicate that educational considerations may be of prime importance when choosing such an alternative to capital-intensive transport. By raising the unit cost per donkey by some 20 percent, it would become possible to plan the production of all its parts in such a manner that, as far as possible, each future owner would spend a month or two making and understanding his machine and would be able to repair it. With this additional cost it would also be possible to decentralize production into dispersed plants. The added benefits would result not only from including educational costs in the construction process. Even more significantly, a durable motor which practically anyone could learn to repair and which could be used as a plough and pump by somebody who understood it would provide much higher educational benefits than the inscrutable engines of the advanced countries.

Not only the junk but also the supposedly public places of the modern city have become impenetrable. In American society, children are excluded from most things and places on the grounds that they are private. But even in societies which have declared an end to private property, children are kept away from the same places because they are considered the special domain of professionals and dangerous to the uninitiated. Since the last generation the railroad yard has become as inaccessible as the fire station. Yet with a little ingenuity, it should not be difficult to provide for safety in such places. To deschool the artifacts of education will require making the artifacts and processes available—and recognizing their educational value. Certainly, some workers would find it inconvenient to be accessible to learners, but this inconvenience must be balanced against the educational gains.

Private cars could be banned from Manhattan. Five years ago, it was unthinkable. Now, certain New York streets are closed off at odd hours, and this trend will probably continue. Indeed most cross streets should be closed to automotive traffic and parking should be forbidden everywhere. In a city opened up to people, teaching materials which are now locked up in storerooms and laboratories could be dispersed into independently operated storefront depots which children and adults could visit without the danger of being run over.

If the goals of learning were no longer dominated by schools and schoolteachers, the market for learners would be much more various and the definition of "educational artifacts" would be less restrictive. There could be tool shops, libraries, laboratories, and gaming rooms. Photolabs and offset presses would allow neighborhood newspapers to flourish. Some storefront learning centers could contain viewing booths for closed-circuit television; others could feature office equipment for use and for repair. The jukebox or the record player would be commonplace, with some specializing in classical music, others in international folk tunes, others in jazz. Film clubs would compete with each other and with commerical television. Museum outlets could be networks for circulating exhibits of works of art, both old and new, originals and reproductions, perhaps administered by the various metropolitan museums.

The professional personnel needed for this network would be much more like custodians, museum guides, or reference librarians than like teachers. From the corner biology store, they could refer their clients to the shell collection in the museum or indicate the next showing of biology videotapes in a certain viewing booth. They could furnish guides for pest control, diet, and other kinds of preventive medicine. They could refer those who needed advice to "elders" who could provide it.

Two distinct approaches can be taken to financing a network of "learning objects." A community could determine a maximum budget for this purpose and arrange for all parts of the network to be open to all visitors at reasonable hours. Or the community could decide to provide citizens with limited entitlements, according to their age group, which would give them special access to certain materials which are both costly and scarce, while leaving other, simpler materials available to everyone.

Finding resources for material made specifically for education is only one—and perhaps the least costly—aspect in building an educational world. The money now spent on the sacred paraphernalia of the school ritual can be freed to provide all citizens with greater access to the real life of the city. Special tax incentives could be granted to those who employed children between the ages of eight and fourteen for a couple of hours each day if the conditions of employment were humane ones. We should return to the tradition of the bar mitzvah or confirmation. By this I mean we should first restrict, and later eliminate, the disenfranchisement of the young and permit a boy of twelve to become a man fully responsible for his participation in the life of the community. Many "school age" people know more about their neighborhood than social workers or councilmen. Of course, they also ask more embarrassing questions and propose solutions which threaten the bureaucracy. They should be allowed to come of age so that they could put their knowledge and fact-finding ability to work in the service of a popular government.

Until recently the dangers of school were easily underestimated in comparison with the dangers of an apprenticeship in the police force, the fire department, or the entertainment industry. It was easy to justify schools at least as a means to protect youth. Often this argument no longer hoids. I recently visited a Methodist church in Harlem occupied by a group of armed Young Lords in protest against the death of Julio Rodan, a Puerto Rican youth found hanged in his prison cell. I knew the leaders of the group who had spent a semester in Cuernavaca. When I wondered why one of them, Juan, was not among them, I was told that he had "gone back on heroin and to the state university."

Planning, incentives, and legislation can be used to unlock the educational potential within our society's huge investment in plants and equipment. Full access to educational objects will not exist so long as business firms are allowed to combine the legal protections which the Bill of Rights reserves to the privacy of individuals with the economic power conferred upon them by their millions of customers and thousands of employees, stockholders, and suppliers. Much of the world's know-how and most of its productive processes and equipment are locked within the walls of business firms, away from their customers, employees, and stockholders, as well as from the general public, whose laws and facilities allow them to function. Money now spent on advertising in capitalist countries could be redirected toward education in and by General Electric, NBC-TV, or the Budweiser beer company. That is, the plants and offices should be reorganized so that their daily operations can be more accessible to the public in ways that will make learning possible; and indeed ways might be found to pay the companies for the learning people acquire from them.

An even more valuable body of scientific objects and data may be withheld from general access—and even from qualified scientists—under the guise of national security. Until recently science was the one forum which functioned like an anarchist's dream. Each man capable of doing research had more or less the same opportunity of access to its tools and to a hearing of the community of peers. Now bureaucratization and organization have placed much of science beyond public reach. Indeed, what used to be an international network of scientific information has been splintered into an arena of competing teams. The members, as well as the artifacts of the scientific community, have been locked into national and corporate programs oriented toward practical achievement, to the radical impoverishment of the men who support these nations and corporations.

In a world which is controlled and owned by nations and corporations, only limited access to educational objects will ever be possible. But increased access to those objects which can be shared for educational purposes may enlighten us enough to help us to break through these ultimate political barriers. Public schools transfer control over the educational uses of objects from private to professional hands. The institutional inversion of schools could empower the individual to reclaim the right to use them for education. A truly public kind of ownership might begin to emerge if private or corporate control over the educational aspect of "things" was brought to the vanishing point.

Skill Exchanges

A guitar teacher, unlike a guitar, can be neither classified in a museum nor owned by the public nor rented from an educational warehouse. Teachers of skills belong to a different class of resources from objects needed to learn a skill. This is not to say that they are indispensable in every case. I can not only rent a guitar but also taped guitar lessons and illustrated chord charts, and with these things I can teach myself to play the guitar. Indeed, this arrangement might have advantages—if the available tapes are better than the available teachers. Or if the only time I have for learning the guitar is late at night or if the tunes I wish to play are unknown in my country. Or I might be shy and prefer to fumble along in privacy.

Skill teachers must be listed and contacted through a different kind of channel from that of things. A thing is available at the bidding of the user—or could be—whereas a person formally becomes a skill resource only when he consents to do so, and he can also restrict time, place, and method as he chooses.

Skill teachers must also be distinguished from peers from whom one would learn. Peers who wish to pursue a common inquiry must start from common interests and abilities; they get together to exercise or improve a skill they share: basketball, dancing, constructing a campsite, or discussing the next election. The first transmission of a skill, on the other hand, involves bringing together someone who has the skill and someone who does not have it and wants to acquire it.

A "skill model" is a person who possesses a skill and is willing to demonstrate its practice. A demonstration of this kind is frequently a necessary resource for a potential learner. Modern inventions permit us to incorporate demonstration into tape, film, or chart; yet one would hope personal demonstration will remain in wide demand, especially in communication skills. Some 10,000 adults have learned Spanish at our center at Cuernavaca—mostly highly motivated persons who wanted to acquire near-native fluency in a second language. When they are faced with a choice between carefully programmed instruction in a lab or drill sessions with two other students and a native speaker following a rigid routine, most choose the second.

For most widely shared skills, a person who demonstrates the skill is the only human resource we ever need or get. Whether in speaking or driving, in cooking or in the use of communication equipment, we are often barely conscious of formal instruction and learning, especially after our first experience of the materials in question. I see no reason why other complex skills, such as the mechanical aspects of surgery and playing the fiddle, of reading or the use of directories and catalogues, could not be learned in the same way.

A well-motivated student who does not labor under a specific handicap often needs no further human assistance than can be provided by someone who can demonstrate on demand how to do what the learner wants to learn to do. The demand made of skilled people that before demonstrating their skill they be certified as pedagogues is a result of the insistence that people learn either what they do not want to know or that all people—even those with a special handicap—learn certain things at a given moment in their lives, and preferably under specified circumstances.

What makes skills scarce on the present educational market is the institutional requirement that those who can demonstrate them may not do so unless they are given public trust through a certificate. We insist that those who help others acquire a skill should also know how to diagnose learning difficulties and be able to motivate people to aspire to learn skills. In short, we demand that they be pedagogues. People who can demonstrate skills will be plentiful as soon as we learn to recognize them outside the teaching profession.

Where princelings are being taught, the parents' insistence that the teacher and the person with skills be combined in one person is understandable, if no longer defensible. But for all parents to aspire to have Aristotle for their Alexander is obviously self-defeating. The person who can both inspire students and demonstrate a technique is so rare, and so hard to recognize, that even princelings more often get a sophist than a true philosopher.

A demand for scarce skills can be quickly filled even if there are only small numbers of people to demonstrate them; but such people must be easily available. During the forties, radio repairmen, most of them with no schooling in their work, were no more than two years behind radios in penetrating the interior of Latin America. There they stayed until transistor radios, which are cheap to purchase and impossible to repair, put them out of business. Technical schools now fail to accomplish what repairmen of equally useful, more durable radios could do as a matter of course.

Converging self-interests now conspire to stop a man from sharing his skill. The man who has the skill profits from its scarcity and not from its reproduction. The teacher who specializes in transmitting the skill profits from the artisan's unwillingness to launch his own apprentice into the field. The public is indoctrinated to believe that skills are valuable and reliable only if they are the result of formal schooling. The job market depends on making skills scarce and on keeping them scarce, either by proscribing their unauthorized use and transmission or by making things which can be operated and repaired only by those who have access to tools or information which are kept scarce.

Schools thus produce shortages of skilled persons. A good example is the diminishing number of nurses in the United States, owing to the rapid increase of four-year B.S. programs in nursing. Women from poorer families, who would formerly have enrolled in a two- or three-year program, now stay out of the nursing profession altogether.

Insisting on the certification of teachers is another way of keeping skills scarce. If nurses were encouraged to train nurses, and if nurses were employed on the basis of their proven skill at giving injections, filling out charts, and giving medicine, there would soon be no lack of trained nurses. Certification now tends to abridge the freedom of education by converting the civil right to share one's knowledge into the privilege of academic freedom, now conferred only on the employees of a school. To guarantee access to an effective exchange of skills, we need legislation which generalizes academic freedom. The right to teach any skill should come under the protection of freedom of speech. Once restrictions on teaching are removed, they will quickly be removed from learning as well.

The teacher of skills needs some inducement to grant his services to a pupil. There are at least two simple ways to begin to channel public funds to noncertified teachers. One way would be to institutionalize the skill exchange by creating free skill centers open to the public. Such centers could and should be established in industrialized areas, at least for those skills which are fundamental prerequisites for entering certain apprenticeships—such skills as reading, typing, keeping accounts, foreign languages, computer programming and number manipulation, reading special languages such as that of electrical circuits, manipulation of certain machinery, etc. Another approach would be to give certain groups within the population educational currency good for attendance at skill centers where other clients would have to pay commercial rates.

A much more radical approach would be to create a "bank" for skill exchange. Each citizen would be given a basic credit with which to acquire fundamental skills. Beyond that minimum, further credits would go to those who earn them by teaching, whether they serve as models in organized skill centers or do so privately at home or on the playground. Only those who have taught others for an equivalent amount of time would have a claim on the time of more advanced teachers. An entirely new elite would be promoted, an elite of those who earn their education by sharing it.

Should parents have the right to earn skill-credit for their children? Since such an arrangement would give further advantage to the privileged classes, it might be offset by granting a larger credit to the underprivileged. The operation of a skill exchange would depend on the existence of agencies which would facilitate the development of directory information and assure its free and inexpensive use. Such an agency might also provide supplementary services of testing and certification and might help to enforce the legislation required to break up and prevent monopolistic practices.

Fundamentally, the freedom of a universal skill exchange must be guaranteed by laws which prevent discrimination only on the basis of tested skills and not on the basis of educational pedigree. Such a guarantee inevitably requires public control over tests which may be used to qualify persons for the job market. Otherwise, it would be possible to surreptitiously reintroduce complex batteries of tests at the work place itself which would serve for social selection. Much could be done to make skill testing objective, e.g., allowing only the operation of specific machines or systems to be tested. Tests of typing (measured according to speed, number of errors, and whether or not the typist can work from dictation), operation of an accounting system or of a hydraulic crane, driving, coding into COBOL, etc., can easily be made objective.

In fact, many of the true skills which are of practical importance can be so tested. And for the purposes of manpower-management, a test of a current skill level is much more useful than the information that a person—twenty years ago—satisfied his teacher in a curriculum where typing, stenography, and accounting were taught. The very need for official skill testing can, of course, be questioned: I personally believe that freedom from undue hurt to a man's reputation through labeling is better guaranteed by restricting than by forbidding tests of competence.

Peer Matching

At their worst, schools gather classmates into the same room and subject them to the same sequence of treatment in math, citizenship, and spelling. At their best, they permit each student to choose one of a limited number of courses. In any case, groups of peers form around the goals of teachers. A desirable educational system would let each person specify the activity for which he seeks a peer.

School does offer children an opportunity to escape their homes and meet new friends. But, at the same time, this process indoctrinates children with the idea that they should select their friends from among those with whom they are put together. Providing the young from their earliest age with invitations to meet, evaluate, and seek out others would prepare them for a lifelong interest in seeking new partners for new endeavors.

A good chess player is always glad to find a close match, and one novice to find another. Clubs serve their purpose. People who want to discuss specific books or articles would probably pay to find discussion partners. People who want to play games, go on excursions, build fish tanks, or motorize bicycles will go to considerable lengths to find peers. The reward for their efforts is finding those peers. Good schools try to bring out the common interests of their students registered in the same program. The inverse of school would be an institution which increases the chances that persons who at a given moment share the same specific interest could meet—no matter what else they have in common.

Skill teaching does not provide equal benefits for both parties as does the matching of peers. The teacher of skills, as I have pointed out, must usually be offered some incentive beyond the rewards of teaching. Skill teaching is a matter of repeating drills over and over and is, in fact, all the more dreary for those pupils who need it most. A skill exchange needs currency or credits or other tangible incentives in order to operate, even if the exchange itself were to generate a currency of its own. A peer-matching system requires no such incentives, but only a communications network.

Tapes, retrieval-systems, programmed instruction, and reproduction of shapes and sounds tend to reduce the need for recourse to human teachers of many skills; they increase the efficiency of teachers and the number of skills one can pick up in a lifetime. Parallel to this runs an increased need to meet people interested in enjoying the newly acquired skill. A student who has picked up Greek before her vacation would like to discuss—in Greek—Cretan politics when she returns. A Mexican in New York wants to find other readers of the paper *Siempre*—or of "Los Asachados," the most popular political cartoons. Somebody else wants to meet peers who—like himself—would like to increase interest in the work of James Baldwin or of Simón Bolívar.

The operation of a peer-matching network would be simple. The user would identify himself by name and address and describe the activity for which he seeks a peer. A computer would send him back the names and addresses of all those who have inserted the same description. It is amazing that such a simple utility has never been used on a broad scale for publicly valued activity.

In its most rudimentary form, communication between client and computer could be done by return mail. In big cities, typewriter terminals could provide instantaneous responses. The only way to retrieve a name and address from the computer would be to list an activity for which a peer is sought. People using the system would become known only to their potential peers.

A complement to the computer could be a network of bulletin boards and classified newspaper ads, listing the activities for which the computer could not produce a match. No names would have to be given. Interested readers would then introduce their names into the system. A publicly supported peer-match network might be the only way to guarantee the right of free assembly and to train people in the exercise of this most fundamental civic activity.

The right of free assembly has been politically recognized and culturally accepted. We should now understand that this right is curtailed by laws that make some forms of assembly obligatory. This is especially the case with institutions which conscript according to age group, class, or sex, and which are very time consuming. The army is one example. School is an even more outrageous one.

To deschool means to abolish the power of one person to oblige another person to attend a meeting. It also means recognizing the right of any person, of any age or sex, to call a meeting. This right has been drastically diminished by the institutionalization of meetings. "Meeting" originally referred to the result of an individual's act of gathering. Now it refers to the institutional produce of some agency.

The ability of service institutions to acquire clients has far outgrown the ability of individuals to be heard independently of institutional media, which respond to individuals only if they are salable news. Peer-matching facilities should be available for individuals who want to bring people together as easily as the village bell called the villagers to council. School buildings—of doubtful value for conversion to other uses—could often serve this purpose.

The school system, in fact, may soon face a problem which churches have faced before: what to do with surplus space emptied by the defection of the faithful. Schools are as difficult to sell as temples. One way to provide for their continued use would be to give over the space to people from the neighborhood. Each could state what he would do in the classroom and when, and a bulletin board would bring the available programs to the attention of the inquirers. Access to "class" would be free or purchased with educational vouchers. The "teacher" could even be paid according to the number of pupils whom he could attract for any full two-hour period. I can imagine that very young leaders and great educators would be the two types most prominent in such a system. The same approach could be taken toward higher education. Students could be furnished with educational vouchers which entitle them for ten hours yearly private consultation with the teacher of their choice and, for the rest of their learning, depend on the library, the peer-matching network, and apprenticeships.

We must, of course, recognize the probability that such public matching devices would be abused for exploitative and immoral purposes, just as the telephone and the mails have been so abused. As with those networks, there must be some protection. I have proposed elsewhere a matching system which would allow only pertinent printed information plus the name and address of the inquirer to be used.(3) Such a system would be virtually foolproof against abuse. Other arrangements could allow the addition of any book, film, TV program, or other item quoted from a special catalogue. Concern with the dangers should not make us lose sight of the far greater benefits.

Some who share my concern for free speech and assembly will argue that peer matching is an artificial means of bringing people together and would not be used by the poor—who most need it. Some people get genuinely agitated when mention is made of creating ad hoc encounters which are not rooted in the life of a local community. Others react when mention is made of using a computer to sort and match client-identified interests. People cannot be drawn together in such an impersonal manner, they say. Common inquiry must be rooted in a history of shared experience at many levels and must grow out of this experience—or in the development of neighborhood institutions, for example.

I sympathize with these objections, but I think they miss my point as well as their own. In the first place, the return to neighborhood life as the primary center of creative expression might actually work against the reestablishment of neighborhoods as political units. Centering demands on the neighborhood may, in fact, neglect an important liberating aspect of urban life—the ability of a person to participate simultaneously in several peer groups. Also, there is an important sense in which people who have never lived together in a physical community may have occasionally far more experiences to share than those who have known each other from childhood. The great religions have always recognized the importance of far-off encounters, and the faithful have always found freedom through them: pilgrimage, monasticism, the mutual support of temples and sanctuaries reflect this awareness. Peer matching could significantly help in making explicit the many potential but suppressed communities of the city.

Local communities are valuable. They are also a vanishing reality as men progressively let service institutions define their circles of social relationship. Milton Kotler in his recent book has shown that the imperialism of "downtown" deprives the neighborhood of its political significance.(4) The protectionist attempt to resurrect the neighborhood as a cultural unit only supports this bureaucratic imperialism. Far from artificially removing men from their local contexts to join abstract groupings, peer matching should encourage the restoration of local life to cities from which it is now disappearing. A man who recovers his initiative to call his fellows into meaningful conversation may cease to settle for being separated from them by office protocol or suburban etiquette. Having once seen that doing things together depends on deciding to do so, men may even insist that their local communities become more open to creative political exchange.

We must recognize that city life tends to become immensely costly, as city dwellers must be taught to rely for every one of their needs on complex institutional services. It is extremely expensive to keep it even minimally livable. Peer matching in the city could be a first step toward breaking down the dependence of citizens on bureaucratic civic services. . . .

Professional Educators

As citizens have new choices—new chances for learning—their willingness to seek leadership should increase. We may expect that they will experience more deeply both their own independence and their need for guidance. As they are liberated from manipulation by others, they learn to profit from the discipline others have acquired in a lifetime. Deschooling education should increase—rather than stifle—the search for men with practical wisdom who are willing to sustain the newcomer on his educational adventure. As teachers abandon their claim to be superior informants or skill models, their claim to superior wisdom will begin to ring true.

With an increasing demand for teachers, the supply should also increase. As the schoolmaster vanishes, the conditions arise which should bring forth the vocation of the independent educator. This may seem almost a contradiction in terms, so thoroughly have schools and teachers become complementary. Yet this is exactly what the development of the first three educational exchanges would tend to produce—and what would be required to permit their full exploitation—for parents and other "natural educators" need guidance, individual learners need assistance, and the networks need people to operate them.

Parents need guidance in guiding their children on the road that leads to responsible educational independence. Learners need experienced leadership when they encounter rough terrain. These two needs are quite distinct: the first is a need for pedagogy; the second, for intellectual leadership in all other fields of knowledge. The first calls for knowledge of human learning and of educational resources; the second, for wisdom based on experience in any kind of exploration. Both kinds of experience are indispensable for effective educational endeavor. Schools package these functions into one role and render the independent exercise of any of them if not disreputable at least suspect.

Three types of special educational competence should in fact be distinguished: one to create and operate the kinds of educational exchanges or networks outlined here; another to guide students and parents in the use of these networks; and a third to act as *primus inter pares* in undertaking difficult intellectual exploratory journeys. Only the former two can be conceived of as branches of an independent profession: educational administrators or pedagogical counselors. To design and operate the networks I have been describing would not require many people, but it would require people with the most profound understanding of education and administration, in a perspective quite different from, and even opposed to, that of schools.

While an independent educational profession of this kind would welcome many people whom the schools exclude, it would also exclude many whom the schools qualify. The establishment and operation of educational networks would require some designers and administrators, but not in the numbers or of the type required by the administration of schools. Student discipline, public relations, hiring, supervising, and firing teachers would have neither place nor counterpart in the networks I have been describing. Neither would curriculum making, textbook purchasing, the maintenance of grounds and facilities, or the supervision of interscholastic athletic competition. Nor would child custody, lesson planning, and record keeping, which now take up so much of the time of teachers, figure in the operation of educational networks. Instead the operation of networks would require some of the skills and attitudes now expected from the staff of a museum, a library, an executive employment agency, or a maitre d'hotel.

Today's educational administrators are concerned with controlling teachers and students to the satisfaction of others—trustees, legislatures, and corporate executives. Network builders and administrators would have to demonstrate genius at keeping themselves, and others, out of people's way, at facilitating encounters of students, skill models, educational leaders, and educational objects. Many persons now attracted to teaching are profoundly authoritarian and would not be able to assume this task: building educational exchanges would mean making it easy for people— especially the young—to pursue goals which might contradict the ideals of the traffic manager who makes the pursuit possible. Pedagogues, in an unschooled world, would also come into their own and be able to do what frustrated teachers pretend to pursue today.

If the networks I have described can emerge, the educational path of each student would be his own to follow and, only in retrospect, would it take on the features of a recognizable program. The wise student would periodically seek professional advice: assistance to set a new goal, insight into difficulties encountered, choice between possible methods. Even now, most persons would admit that the important services their teachers have rendered them are such advice or counsel, given at a chance meeting or in a tutorial.

While network administrators would concentrate primarily on the building and maintenance of roads providing access to resources, the pedagogue would help the student to find the path which for him could lead fastest to his goal. If a student wants to learn spoken Cantonese from a Chinese neighbor, the pedagogue would be available to judge their proficiency and to help them select the textbook and methods most suitable to their talents, character, and the time available for study. He can counsel the would-be airplane mechanic on finding the best places for apprenticeship. He can recommend books to somebody who wants to find challenging peers to discuss African history. Like the network administrator, the pedagogical counselor conceives of himself as a professional educator. Access to either could be gained by individuals through the use of educational vouchers.

The role of the educational initiator or leader, the master or "true" leader, is somewhat more elusive than that of the professional administrator or pedagogue. This is so because leadership is itself hard to define. In practice, an individual is a leader if people follow his initiative and become apprentices in his progressive discoveries. . . .

The relationship of master and disciple is not restricted to intellectual discipline. It has its counterpart in the arts, in physics, in religion, in psychoanalysis, and in pedagogy. It fits mountainclimbing, silverworking and politics, cabinetmaking and personnel administration. What is common to all true master-pupil relationships is the awareness both share that their relationship is literally priceless—and in very different ways a privilege for both. . . .

To rely for true intellectual leadership on the desire of gifted people to provide it is obviously necessary even in our society, but it could not be made into a policy now. We must first construct a society in which personal acts themselves reacquire a value higher than that of making things and manipulating people.(5) In such a society exploratory, inventive, creative teaching would logically be counted among the most desirable forms of leisurely "unemployment." But we do not have to wait until the advent of Utopia. Even now one of the most important consequences of deschooling and the establishment of peer-matching facilities would be the initiative which "masters" could take to assemble congenial disciples. It would also—as we have seen—provide ample opportunity for potential disciples to share information or to select a master.

Schools are not the only institutions which pervert professions by packaging roles. Hospitals render home care increasingly impossible—and then justify hospitalization as a benefit to the sick. At the same time the doctor's legitimacy and ability to work increasingly come to depend on his association with a hospital, even though he is still less totally dependent on it than are teachers on schools. The same could be said about courts, which overcrowd their calendars as new transactions acquire legal solemnity—and thus delay justice. Or it could be said about churches, which succeed in making a captive profession out of a free vocation. The result in each case is scarce service at higher cost; and greater income to the less competent members of the profession.

So long as the older professions monopolize superior income and prestige, it is difficult to reform them. The profession of the schoolteacher should be easier to reform, and not only because it is of more recent origin. The educational profession now claims a comprehensive monopoly; it claims the exclusive competence to apprentice not only its own novices but those of other professions as well. This overexpansion renders it vulnerable to any profession which would reclaim the right to teach its own apprentices. Schoolteachers can be overwhelmingly badly paid and frustrated by the tight control of the school system. The most enterprising and gifted among them would probably find more congenial work, more independence, and even higher incomes by specializing as skill models, network administrators, or guidance specialists.

Finally, the dependence of the registered student on the certified teacher can be broken more easily than his dependence on other professionals—for instance, that of a hospitalized patient on his doctor. If schools ceased to be compulsory, teachers who find their satisfaction in the exercise of pedagogical authority in the classroom would be left only with pupils who are attracted by their style. The disestablishment of our present professional structure could begin with the dropping out of the schoolteacher.

The disestablishment of schools will inevitably happen—and it will happen surprisingly fast. It cannot be retarded very much longer and it is hardly necessary to vigorously promote it, for this is being done now. What is worthwhile is to try to orient it in a hopeful direction for it could take place in two diametrically opposed ways.

The first would be the expansion of the mandate of the pedagogue and his increasing control over society, even outside school. With the best of intentions and simply by expanding the rhetoric now used in school, the present crisis in the schools could provide educators with an excuse to use all the networks of contemporary society to funnel their messages to us—for our own good. Deschooling, which we cannot stop, could mean the advent of a "brave new world" dominated by well-intentioned administrators of programmed instruction.

On the other hand, the growing awareness on the part of governments, as well as of employers, taxpayers, enlightened pedagogues, and school administrators that graded curricular teaching for certification has become harmful could offer large masses of people an extraordinary opportunity: that of preserving the right of equal access to the tools both of learning and of sharing with others what they know or believe. But this would require that the educational revolution be guided by certain goals:

1) To liberate access to things by abolishing the control which persons and institutions now exercise over their educational values

2) To liberate the sharing of skills by guaranteeing freedom to teach or exercise them on request

3) To liberate the critical and creative resources of people by returning to individual persons the ability to call and hold meetings: an ability now increasingly monopolized by institutions which claim to speak for the people

4) To liberate the individual from the obligation to shape his expectations to the services offered by an established profession by providing him with the opportunity to draw on the experience of his peers and to entrust himself to the teacher, guide, adviser, or healer of his choice

Inevitably deschooling of society blurs the distinctions between economics, education, and politics on which the stability of the present world order and the stability of nations now rests.

In addition to the tentative conclusions of the Carnegie Commission reports, the last year has brought forth a series of important documents which show that responsible people are becoming aware of the fact that schooling for certification cannot continue to be counted upon as the central educational device of a modern society. Julius Nyere of Tanzania has announced plans to integrate education with the life of the village. In Canada, the Wright Commission on postsecondary education has reported that no known system of formal education could provide equal opportunities for the citizens of Ontario. The president of Peru has accepted the recommendation of his commission on education, which proposes to abolish free schools in favor of free educational opportunities provided throughout life. In fact he is reported to have insisted that this program proceed slowly at first in order to keep teachers in school and out of the way of true educators.

What has happened is that some of the boldest and most imaginative public leaders find their insights into school failures matching those of radical free spirits (for example, Paul Goodman) who only a few years ago were seen as anarchic. More programmatic radicals, on the other hand, often simply seek to obtain control over schools and other teaching media and thus only strengthen the certifiction system.

The alternative to social control through the schools is the voluntary participation in society through networks which provide access to all its resources for learning. In fact, these networks now exist but they are rarely used for educational purposes. The crisis of schooling, if it is to have any positive consequence, will inevitably lead to their incorporation into the educational process.

Notes

1. Ivan Illich, "Schooling: The Ritual of Progress," *New York Review* (December 3, 1970).
2. Documentation on the construction, testing, and use of such machines is now in preparation at CIDOC.
3. Ivan Illich, "Why We Must Abolish Schooling," *New York Review* (July 2, 1970).
4. Milton Kotler, *Neighborhood Governments: The Local Foundations of Political Life* (Indianapolis, Ind.: The Bobbs-Merrill Co., Inc., 1969).
5. For a fuller discussion of these distinctions, see my book, *DeSchooling Society* (New York: Harper & Row, 1971).

V Responses

A View from Within

Philip W. Jackson

How true—when you happen not to be a school-teacher yourself—how true those oft-quoted lines sound—

Under a cruel eye outworn
The little ones spend the day
in sighing and dismay!

But when you yourself are the cruel eye outworn, you realize that there is another side to the picture.*

George Orwell, *The Clergyman's Daughter*

Many of us who work in schools, save those situated in urban ghettos, are becoming increasingly reluctant these days to wander outside the shelter of our institutions. And small wonder! Within the classrooms over which we preside and along the corridors through which we pass, the atmosphere is pleasant, if not exactly peaceful. There is the customary confusion that surrounds the processes of teaching and learning, of course, and more than enough discomfort from time to time. But, by and large, a sense of satisfaction and accomplishment accompanies much that goes on within our not-so-ivied walls.

From across the street, however, the view is quite different. At that distance the appearance of internal calm and the business-as-usual attitude on the part of the practitioner cannot help but be interpreted as signs of callous indifference. For outside our schools the air is thick with the cries of critics.

This situation is not exactly new, we know. Schools have long been the favorite targets of critics, both from the outside and from

*From George Orwell, *The Clergyman's Daughter* (New York: Harcourt Brace Jovanovich, Inc., 1935), p. 271. Reprinted with permission of the publisher.

within. And, given the importance of education and the variety of interpretations to be put upon it, such a condition would be surprising if it were otherwise. But, though historically commonplace, attacks upon our schools do vary from time to time in both their magnitude and their substance. At present the volume is unusually high and we find ourselves in the midst of a particularly intensive barrage of catcalls, complaints, diagnoses, and freely proffered remedies for our educational ills. Moreover, in recent months, as the four articles in the first section of this monograph illustrate, the strategy of the critics has taken a new turn.

Until quite recently the desirability of schools and of compulsory attendance by the young were more or less taken for granted by friend and foe alike. The goal of both, even of those who were most unhappy with the status quo, was not to do away with our schools as we now know them, but somehow to improve their operation. Some critics contented themselves with the detection of faults in our present system, leaving their correction in the hands of professional educators. Others went on to spell out in considerable detail their own plans for educational reform. But whether or not they offered specific remedies, most critics, until quite recently, operated on the assumption that our schools, as such, would endure the reformers' zeal. There would be changes, to be sure, but schoolhouses and classrooms and teachers and lessons and some form of compulsory attendance would somehow still be there when the dust settled.

Now, judging from the articles in this monograph, the critic's voice is becoming harsher and his ideas more radical. His tools seem to be changing from hammers and saws to battering rams and bulldozers—from instruments of construction to ones of destruction. Moreover, as these new land-clearance engineers rumble toward the schools, an increasingly large crowd of onlookers seems to be on hand to cheer them along and to enjoy the sport.

Why such radical action is necessary is, of course, the most important question to be asked. The only acceptable answer to that question (aside from acknowledging that some people derive perverse pleasure from the act of destruction for its own sake) is to claim that our schools today are so hopelessly bad that nothing can be done to salvage them. This being so, it follows that no matter what takes their place, the resultant arrangement is bound to be an improvement over what we now have.

Some form of this contention, with various elaborations and qualifications, is advanced by almost all the radical critics of our schools. As Goodman puts it, "Only a small fraction, the 'academically talented'—about 15 percent according to James Conant—thrive in schools without being bored or harmed by them." Reimer takes Goodman's assertion one step further by claiming that, "The school system also fails in part to educate most of its nominally successful students, stultifying, rather than nurturing, their lifetime capacity and desire for learning." Illich is quoted in a national magazine as saying, "Preventive concentration camps for predelinquents would be a logical improvement over the school system." Other critics, though less extreme, echo similar sentiments.

Now such charges are serious indeed. If true, they would certainly justify a battering-ram approach to educational reform. But the seriousness of such a consequence also demands caution. Before taking up the cudgels of attack, we need to understand how Goodman, Reimer, Illich, and others arrive at such a devastating verdict. For, if it should turn out that their verdict is unjustified, we must not hesitate to turn our backs on it, no matter how unfashionable it may be to support the Establishment and no matter how unpopular such a stance may make us at the weekend cocktail party.

If we turn to the search for facts, a disenchantment with the radical critics is quick in coming. For even under the most liberal definition of proof, there is precious little to substantiate the basic premise on which the deschooling argument rests. That is, there is no solid evidence to support the blanket assertion that schools in our society are failing to educate our children, much less that they are actually doing them harm. This is not to say that there are not students—too many, we know—for whom such a charge is true. We hardly need proof, for example, to convince us that life in many of our inner-city high schools is miserable indeed. We are also painfully aware that a sizable number of our middle-class adolescents are being turned off by their school experience. But to move from such knowledge, lamentable as it is, to a general indictment of our entire school system is to take a giant step indeed, totally unwarranted by the evidence at hand.

Not only is there no basis for concluding that public school pupils across the land are gnashing their teeth in despair and rattling their tin cups against the bars of the classroom in protest against the injustices they are suffering but the few scraps of evidence that do exist point to quite the opposite conclusion. From the middle 1930's to the present day, almost every systematic study of educational attitudes that has been undertaken has revealed the vast majority of students, from the middle grades onward, to be surprisingly content with their school experience. Apparently, almost four out of five students, if asked directly, would confess a liking for school, with all its faults.

Such evidence must of course be taken with a grain of salt, for it can always be argued that the majority of students are content with school simply because they have little else with which to compare it (save summer vacation). Nonetheless, even if accepted with great reservation, it is difficult to reconcile the few facts that do exist with the iconoclastic condemnations of the deschoolers.

In addition to basing their arguments on scant evidence concerning the state of our schools today, the proponents of deschooling seem curiously lacking in historical perspective. Though educational progress, like human progress in general, has clearly had its ups and downs throughout history and leaves no reason to believe that future improvement is inevitable, it does seem true that schools in our country, and probably in the entire Western world, are superior in many respects to those that existed a century or two ago. They serve a larger segment of our citizenry, they follow curricula that are more varied and better suited to the future needs of our students than was true in the past, and they are staffed by teachers who, on the whole, are better educated and more humane in their dealings with children than were their predecessors a few generations back. Gone are the hickory stick, the rapped knuckles, and the dunce's cap, together with the heavy reliance on rote memory, the rigidity of the recitation method, and the bolted-down desk. Some of the educational practices that have taken their place leave much to be desired, it is true, but with all of our present educational shortcomings, it is difficult to avoid the terribly smug conclusion that our schools are better today than they have ever been before.

Such smugness should not be accompanied by complacency, however, for whatever progress has been made has required hard work, and there is much yet to be done. Moreover, we have no guarantee that things will not get worse rather than better. Nonetheless, the overall impression of progress, unstable though it may be, does not sit well with the assertion that our present system is one great failure. Faced with such a charge, one is tempted to say to the critic, "If you think our schools are bad now, you should have seen them in your grandfather's day!"

Much as it might dampen the critic's flame, a calm look at what goes on in our classrooms reveals them to be neither Dickensian nor Orwellian horrors. They are neither prisons, presided over by modern-day Fagins who take delight in twisting ears and otherwise torturing children, nor are they gigantic Skinner boxes, designed to produce well-conditioned automatons who will uncritically serve the state. Anyone who believes in the truth of such fictions should take a few days off to visit his local schools. Should he find the fiction to be matched by reality, he would indeed have reason to seek change by whatever means are available. But anyone who, with or without such personal experience, proceeds to argue that such is the state of all or even most of our schools, must either be misinformed or irresponsible.

Even if we overlook available evidence, both contemporary and historical, and accept the conclusion that our schools are in such a sorry state as to warrant abolishing them, we must ask what will happen when their doors are closed for good. What, in other words, will our youth be doing during the hours normally spent in school?

The answer to that question is a bit vague, to say the least, in the writings of most critics, but usually it is assumed that school-age children, free from the artificial demands of the classroom, will be enthusiastically engaged in learning (Goodman calls it "incidental learning") through contact with real-life situations. Guided by nothing more than natural curiosity and an instinctual love for learning, our children will presumably wander over the streets and fields of our land, gathering rosebuds of wisdom along the way. Adults, gladdened by the sight of these wandering scholars, will hail them as they pass and will invite them into the shops and factories and offices and hospitals, where they will become apprentices and learn at the feet of their elders those skills and trades that will equip them to take a productive place within our society.

Of course, no self-respecting critic would accept this caricature of the postschool era, but the romantic idealism contained in such an image is strongly evident in the imagination of many who criticize our current educational scene. However, when they begin to muse on how this Whitmanesque ideal might be achieved, something very much like the structure of our present schools, or at least the best of them, begins to emerge.

The chief difficulty with many advocates of the incidental-learning position is their failure to distinguish between learning and education. For most of us, incidental learning of one sort or another is indeed occurring all the time. As I glance up from my desk at this very moment, for example, I have just "learned" that my neighbor is about to mow his lawn! But education obviously involves much more than the accumulation of such fortuitous bits of information. It involves learning that is prescribed and planned and guided. Humans can indeed educate themselves, but experience seems to show that the process occurs more effectively with outside help. It was with this realization that the idea of a teacher was born. When our forebearers began to come to grips with the fact that not all adults could spend their time at such a pursuit, the notion of a school was in the offing.

Doubtlessly, there *are* children who, freed from the formal demands of schools and with a minimum of adult guidance, would set about the laborious task of educating themselves. But whether all or most children, if pressed to do so, would turn out to be such self-motivated learners is indeed doubtful. Moreover, there is at least some reason to believe that those who would suffer most from the absence of classroom constraints and teacher guidance would be those children who already exhibit signs of educational impoverishment. Thus, left largely to their own devices, our out-of-school learners would likely behave in ways that would result in exaggerating the cleavages that already separate social class groups within our society.

Finally, even if educators or their critics wanted to set children free to learn on their own without the confines of a school and all the restrictions it implies, there is ample reason to believe that parents and other adults in our society would not stand for it. Like it or not, our schools presently perform a custodial function as well as an educational one. Parents, particularly those of young children, simply do not want their offspring to be unsupervised during much of the day. We could, of course, substitute compulsory day-care centers or neighborhood clubs for compulsory schools, but, when we consider such alternatives, they begin to look not all that different from what used to go on in the empty schoolhouse down the block.

In summary, the arguments of the deschoolers suffer from two serious flaws. They begin with a false picture of how bad things are in our schools today, and they end with a highly romanticized notion of what might be substituted for our present educational system.

Meanwhile, back in the classroom, there is a lot of work to be done. Our inner-city schools, particularly high schools, *are* disaster areas; too many of our students, particularly our adolescents, *are* being turned off by their school experience; the bureaucratic structure of our schools, particularly our larger ones, *is* more abrasive than it needs to be; our graded system *is* too rigid and requires loosening up; our teacher certification laws *are* shamefully archaic and prevent many good people from taking their place in the classroom; our schools *do* need to be linked more imaginatively to the communities they serve.

These *are* serious problems, badly in need of solution. The crucial question is whether their solution requires the abandonment or the overthrow of the entire system. To answer that question, we must consider what is *right* about our schools as well as what is wrong with them. In balance, at least as seen from the inside, the pros clearly outweigh the cons.

VI

The Educational
Future of the Incipient
Revolution: Total
Manipulation or Faith
in Man's Ability to
Choose?

John Ohliger

This paper will focus on the Illich essay with some reference to the proposal edited by Reimer (which by now is quite outdated by later writings). Goodman's contradictory insights and changing frames of reference simply confuse me. Goodman's great value, it seems to me, is as a critic of other men's ideas and work. Illich pays tribute to Goodman for performing the critical function so effectively with his own work in the introduction to his new book. (1) Bereiter's piece impresses me as a partial proposal at the beginning of the road to the Illich-Reimer goals.

After agreeing to do this reaction paper, I began to have mixed feelings. What does the NSSE have in mind? Is this conventionally respectable old organization interested in exploring fully the implications of proposals for deschooling, in trying to co-opt its proponents or their ideas for the Establishment, or in smothering them in nit-picking pedantic criticism? It's probably the second or third alternatives, but there is always the hopeful chance, slight as it may be, that the society will live up to its name as being devoted to the "study of education," not schools.

One of the main points of the Illich-Reimer view is that new languages should be developed to explore the meanings of the terms *education* and *school* without reference to each other. Such an antidote to the horrendously common assumption that the terms are synonymous is urgently needed. If the book in which this reaction paper appears encourages the growth of such separate languages, it will justify the expenditure of time, effort, and money involved. If not, forget it! It will then be just one more contribution to paper pollution and stimulus overload.

The key assumption I make in writing this paper is that we are in the beginning stages of a vast revolutionary period. The outcome for the individual will either be a world friendly to freedom or a counterrevolutionary, universal prison. We are either on the way up or down. Escalating frustrations, tensions, hypocrisies, and demands make "muddling through" less and less practical.

It is impossible for me to react only to the Illich and Reimer material published here. Having read everything of theirs I could get my hands on, read the works of their mentor Paulo Freire, conducted two graduate seminars on their views, and prepared speeches, articles, book reviews, bibliographies, and essays based on their thoughts, I'm sure that reacting only to these two pieces would result in a paper full of dull textual criticism, minutiae, trivia, and exegesis.

Since this is instead a reaction paper, let me give a few of my gut-level reactions when I first encountered the Illich-Reimer thesis. I experienced a mixture of shock and enthusiasm. I was shocked that I had never before really considered the possibility that schools were unnecessary. Though I had been intensely critical of the school establishment, especially in its relation to adults and adult learning, I had never basically questioned the right of such institutions to exist or to monopolize tax resources for education. Undoubtedly this was so in part because I made my living working for schools and didn't want to face the possible personal consequences of their disestablishment. I still can't fully face those consequences, but at least I can begin to examine them, if only gingerly.

I was enthusiastic about the complete and well-researched rejection by Illich and Reimer of the cruel fiction of childhood. If nothing else, the disappearance from the popular idiom of the stupid question, "What do you want to *be* when you grow up?" would warrant a monument to them. It is clear that once out of infancy, a person *is* and is capable of self-motivated and self-disciplined learning. He deserves to be considered a full person. The term *adult* may not be the best one to apply to a person at any age (after all *adult* is the past participle of the Latin verb "adolescere," and who wants to be the past participle of an adolescent?), but the best connotations of that word should be available to everyone at an early age. Of course, such an approach appeals to my predisposition to adult education. It is extremely rare to find such able thinkers in the adult education camp, in the sense that they reject the obscene concentration of educational resources on "youth." And it is heartening to see that so many of their examples and suggestions deal with the adult "stepchild" area of education. In addition, their devotion, for good nontechnocratic reasons, to "self-directed learning" and "lifelong learning," two much-touted concepts in our field, is happily obvious, even in the brief items reproduced here.

Naturally after discovering such attractive allies, I am prone to resent criticism of them. I make no pretense that my views of the Illich-Reimer critics are unbiased. The most common criticism from my students, my colleagues, and the few writers who have so far commented in print, goes something like this: "We find no fault with the Illich-Reimer analysis of the worldwide school system. It is complete, and the criticisms, generalizations, and characterizations they make are correct and well-expressed. But we just can't go along with their proposals for change. They are not clear cut enough. They leave too many unanswered questions. Their proposals are not demonstrably feasible. Their blueprint for the future simply isn't fully worked out." Whatever we think of Karl Marx, anyone familiar with history must realize that he destroyed forever the argument that complete blueprints of the future are either necessary or desirable.

It seems to me that those who make such criticisms of the Illich-Reimer proposals are just not willing to face up to the resulting implications. They say they agree with it. But do they really? The Illich-Reimer proposals are merely logical, common sense extrapolations of their analysis given one additional ingredient— hope for the future of humans as active doers. In varying degrees, I believe, the critics voicing the above-mentioned remarks have in effect thrown in the towel. As Paulo Freire puts it:

(Some) men are afraid to risk living the future as creative overcoming of the present, which has become old. . . . That is why people today study all the possibilities which the future contains, in order to "domesticate" it and keep it in line with the present, which is what they intend to maintain. . . . That is why there is no genuine hope in those who intend to make the future as something predetermined. Both have a "domesticated" notion of history: the former because they want to stop time; the latter because they are certain about a future they already "know."(2)

On the other hand, there is no doubt that a great deal of intellectual work lies ahead with the challenges Illich and Reimer present. They both recognize this. This is why Illich calls for "counterfoil research to current futurology" on the second page of his latest book.(3)

I am not implying that there are no valid or significant criticisms of their work. Elsewhere I have pointed to what I believe is their unnecessary and incongruous attachment to the market mechanism.(4) But it seems to me that, because of the novel nature of their combination of unusual insights, worthwhile criticism should flow from a careful reading of the corpus of their writings. I am sorry to say I don't think the samples presented in this book are sufficient to even a rudimentary understanding of their thesis. At the very least, Illich's new book, *Deschooling Society,* and Reimer's long *Essay on Alternatives in Education* should be read.(5)

One person who has read Illich and Reimer sufficiently and who provides some thoughtful comment is Edgar Z. Friedenberg. Friedenberg has written:

Proposals for deschooling society and reducing its dependency on formal credentials would indeed, if implemented, liberate children from the humiliating imposition of a constrictive and often foreign style of life, and make it harder to label those who rebelled or resisted as losers. But they would also deny parents who wanted to submit their children to such indoctrination, or children who wanted it for themselves in the interests of "getting somewhere," from using education as a means of social mobility. . . . This does not mean that . . . the elimination of compulsory school (is not a goal) to be zealously sought. It means merely that there are real conflicts of interest in society, and that the better course of action may sometimes be distinguished and supported even though by doing so one advances the interests of a relatively privileged class at the expense of the already disadvantaged.(6)

Of course, Illich is strongly opposed to advancing "the interests of a relatively privileged class at the expense of the already disadvantaged," and he has called for the drastic restructuring of other social institutions as well (medical, social welfare, military, etc.). In addition he has vociferously denied seeking the development of "the new man." This leaves two plausible directions for revision: one, the integration of moves toward institutional revolution, *i.e.,* the combination of deschooling with radical changes in other oppressive institutions, and, two, the overall integration of general institutional revolution with political revolution. So far Illich has concentrated his attention on pointing out the failure of political revolution to accomplish worthwhile change without institutional revolution. It is time now to recognize that the reverse is true as well and to begin to build toward integrated revolution.

Such building of an integrated approach is, of course, a nice intellectual exercise for those of us blessed with the leisure to do so. Even here our work has been anticipated somewhat by Freire's call for "permanent revolution."(7) But the hard work comes, when all the rhetoric is stripped away, in finding a handle—any humanistic handle—to begin valuable and effective revolutionary change. It is here that I believe Illich offers one potentially worthwhile guide.

Though disestablishment of schools is far from enough, it may well be the battlefield for the first moves toward the growth of a society truly fit for modern human habitation. We can criticize Illich's proposals all we like, but I believe we ignore his warnings about the next turn in the road at our peril. Illich believes, and is gathering increasing historical evidence to show, that we are moving inevitably toward the disestablishment of schools. Their failures are simply becoming too evident to too many people: the ritual is being exposed, and as soon as enough people become aware that it is a ritual, the game will be over.

But then what? What follows the loss of the school's monopolistic power? This is the point in time where the greatest attention should be paid to Illich. He sees that deschooling could go in one of two directions. In the article reproduced here (and included in revised form in his new book as Chapter 6, "Learning Webs"), he states:

With the best of intentions and simply by expanding the rhetoric now used in school, the present crisis in the schools could provide educators with an excuse to use all the networks of contemporary society to funnel their messages to us—for our own good. Deschooling, which we cannot stop, could mean the advent of a "brave new world" dominated by well-intentioned administrators of programmed instruction.(8)

At least five times in his new book he points to the horrible alternative that faces us:

If we do not challenge the assumption that valuable knowledge is a commodity which under certain circumstances may be forced into the consumer, society will be increasingly dominated by sinister pseudoschools and totalitarian managers of information. (9)

The other possible direction for deschooling is the one Illich is proposing toward self-directed learning in a society where meaningful choices will be possible for the first time. His pure model is obviously only intended as a series of rough suggestive guidelines. (The Illich essay reproduced here provides a partial view of his proposals.)

The choice is ours. We educators can play a part in the revolutionary leadership that will help to nurture the power of the individual to really choose *what, when, why, how,* and *if* he will learn or *not*; or we can become the lackeys of the "therapeutic Big Brother." If we choose the humanistic path, we must have faith—"faith in the educability of man" (10)—and we must recognize that such faith, as it is fulfilled, will lead inevitably to other types of revolutionary change in political, economic, and other controlling power configurations.

Illich and Reimer have pointed to the need for all-encompassing radical change in society. That Illich is beginning to move strategically toward the need for integrating institutional and political revolution is borne out in these statements in a working draft of one of his latest efforts:

If we formulate principles for alternative institutional (educational) arrangements and an alternative emphasis in the conception of learning, we will also be suggesting principles for a radically alternative political and economic organization. . . . It should be clear that only through the definition of what constitutes a desirable society, arrived at in the meeting of those who are both dispossessed and also disabused of the dream that constantly increasing quanta of consumption can provide them with the joy they seek out of life, can the inversion of institutional arrangement here drafted be put into effect, and, also with it, a technological society which values occupation, intensive work, and leisure over alienation through goods and services. (11)

This paper owes some of its development to work done on a previous publication: *Lifelong Learning or Lifelong Schooling?: A Tentative View of the Ideas of Ivan Illich with a Quotational Bibliography* by John Ohliger and Colleen McCarthy (Syracuse, New York: Syracuse University, Library of Continuing Education, July 1971).

Notes

1. Ivan Illich, *Deschooling Society* (New York: Harper & Row, Publishers, 1971), p. xx.
2. Paulo Friere, "The Adult Literacy Process As Cultural Action for Freedom," *Harvard Educational Review* (May 1970).
3. Illich, *op. cit.* p. 2.
4. John Ohliger and Colleen McCarthy. *Lifelong Learning or Lifelong Schooling?: A Tentative View of the Ideas of Ivan Illich with a Quotational Bibliography* (Syracuse, New York: Syracuse University, Library of Continuing Education, July 1971).
5. Everett Reimer. *An Essay on Alternatives in Education,* 3rd draft, Cidoc Cuaderno No. 1005 (Cuernavaca, Mexico: CIDOC, February 1971). To be published in revised form and possibly with a different title in late 1971 by Doubleday and Company, Inc., Garden City, New York.
6. Edgar Z. Friedenberg, "Bad Blood," *New York Review of Books* (May 20, 1971), p. 10.
7. Paulo Freire, *Pedagogy of the Oppressed* (New York: Herder and Herder, 1970).
8. Illich, *op. cit.* p. 103.
9. *Ibid.*, pp. 49-50.
10. Ivan Illich, *The Institutionalization of Truth* (A videotape of a lecture delivered in the spring of 1970 at York University in Toronto, Canada. For information on availability write to Reg Herman, Managing Editor, *Convergence*, P.O. Box 250, Station F, Toronto 5, Ontario, Canada).
11. Ivan Illich, *The Breakdown of Schools: A Problem or a Symptom?* Working Draft of a Paper for Discussion, CIDOC Doc. A/E 71/308 (Cuer-

navaca, Mexico: CIDOC, April 21, 1971) pp. 13 and 27. (Some of the ideas from this draft have been reworked into a more recent and more generally available article by Illich: "The Alternative to Schooling," *Saturday Review* (June 19, 1971), pp. 44-48, 59-60.

12. My thanks to Joel Rosenberg, Stanley Grabowski, Richard Dodd, Colleen McCarthy, Wilma Parr, David Williams, Timothy Leonard, and Doris Chertow for their critical reading of a draft of this paper and for their helpful suggestions for improvement.

VII

The Romantic Radicals— A Threat to Reform

Mortimer Smith

These are disheartening days for educational reformers, that is, for those who believe that the ills of education and schools can be alleviated by patient and judicious efforts to rectify past mistakes. What is disheartening is that reform threatens to give way to revolution: we are witnessing a determined assault by those who do not want to remold or rebuild the school, but to destroy it. Influenced by the wide publicity given to the revolutionaries' views in newspapers and the popular magazines (where absolutist positions are always welcomed as lively news), one may take the movement for educational revolution too seriously. However, when such a cautious body as the National Society for the Study of Education decides to devote a symposium to the revolution, it may indicate that it is more than a passing fashion.

Before examining the position of the revolutionaries, or romantic radicals, as I have taken to calling them, let me state briefly my own approach to educational change. I believe that the basic structure and many of the procedures of public education are valid and that reform can be accomplished without drastic organizational alterations. I believe that a public system of education is a social convenience and necessity, and that if, by some miracle, we could achieve "deschooling" tomorrow, the resultant chaos would be such that we would immediately have to start bootlegging formal instruction. I believe that schooling, to be efficient, has to be formalized, with required attendance, sequential courses, and schedules. And I believe that the teacher and the taught are not equal partners in the educational process, a process which assumes that the one has something to give that the other does not yet possess. To reiterate, I believe that within this framework of school organization, genuine reforms can be accomplished. Later in this writing I will describe some of these reforms. My present fear is that the Utopian pipe dreams of the romantic radicals will divert us from taking those steps that can result in realizable reform and improvement of the schools.

Using the term *radical* as denoting originality, which is one of its meanings, it can hardly be said that our current revolutionaries are saying anything new about education and schooling. Their message is for the most part derivative, at least as old as Rousseau and *Emile*. What George Santayana said of the French philosopher in his book *Dominations and Powers* can be said of the modern educational radical:

Human society seemed to him a prison, and the prisoners pure equal spirits capable of the most exalted happiness, if only they were left free to wander in couples through a new Garden of Eden as through a landscape of Watteau.

Not only does the radicals' insistence on freedom for the noble savage derive from Rousseau but the philosopher confirms some of the precise doctrines of the new creed. The radicals' dislike of examinations, for example, is echoed in his remark: "Let Emile never be led to compare himself to other children. No rivalries, not even in running, as soon as he begins to have the power of reason." William James quotes this sentiment in his *Talks to Teachers*, where he regrets the effort to banish "marks, distinctions, prizes, and other goals of effort, based on the pursuit of recognized superiority." The modern revolt against "bookishness" is also to be found in *Emile*: "When I get rid of children's lessons, I get rid of the chief cause of their sorrow, namely their books. Reading is the chief curse of childhood, yet it is almost the only occupation you can find for children."

Much of what the radicals have to say was also being said in the 1920's during the heyday of the progressive movement in education. A. S. Neill anticipated many of the ideas in his school Summerhill, which he founded fifty years ago. The impatience with subject matter, the emphasis on the child's needs (now translated as "relevance"), on creativity, and on free expression and free activity versus discipline and a structured program—all these ideas were part of the earlier movement. Our radicals' preoccupation with economic and social aims and with the class struggle carry us back to the 1930's and the *Social Frontier*, to George S. Counts' monograph, *Dare the Schools Build a New Social Order?*, and to the movement for indoctrination of the schools sponsored by such men as Harold Rugg, John L. Childs, Norman Woelfel, and Jesse

M. Newlon. In the radicals' writings there are also touches of the "life adjustment" movement of the 1940's and 1950's, although it must be said that, on the whole, they state their case more persuasively and gracefully than did the rather pedestrian and lackluster educationists who fathered life adjustment.

Illich and Goodman, who share many of the romantic radicals' views, even resurrect the old device the field trip. This is not a trivial matter, for the field trip is at the heart of their scheme of things. Their argument is that the child and young person learn not through formal teaching but from their environment and from doing. (What a nostalgic sound that has! Sometimes it seems as if Illich and Goodman are part of the current movement to romanticize the not-so-distant past. Perhaps "learning by doing" is to take its place along with the revival of old movies, big name bands, and Howdy Doody.)

The learner is to acquire knowledge and skills by poking around in libraries and museums, by watching craftsmen in tool shops, by listening to others speak Spanish. If I read Illich correctly, youth is even going to acquire specialized skills, without prior formal training, simply by watching surgeons and fiddlers in action, a practice bound to set back the clock in medicine and music. Illich has a rather cavalier attitude toward all professionalism and a childlike fath that once we are liberated from manipulation by professional teachers, we will in our wanderings find other "skill-models" in the community. They will show us by example how to repair telephones, become linguists, practice midwifery, or design buildings.

All this will happen because in Illich and Goodman's scheme of things all young people want to learn, and if left to their own devices will seek out the sources of knowledge. Behind this assumption seems to lurk the old notion that learning results only from interest, as well as the idea that all minds are intensely inquiring minds. The idea that there is no learning without prior interest cannot be accepted without a caveat. Many people can testify that in some instances they have become aware of interest only *after* they learned something that had no initial appeal for them. There are many things we would never learn if we had to wait for the spark of interest.

As for the suggestion that the desire to learn is of universal intensity, dropouts who hang around street corners are not notably imbued with it. Illich and Goodman would probably say that they were "turned off" by coercive school practices, but the more likely explanation is that they were cheated by exactly the sort of laissez faire pedagogy the romantics extol. The self-motivated person will want to learn in whatever situation he finds himself, but if the unmotivated majority is to learn in the brave new world of nonschools, its members are going to have to be led to learning, just as they are in the world of conventional schools.

It is important to bear in mind that the ideas of the romantics are not abstract educational theories, ever introduced in the academic marketplace. Except for the notion of total deschooling, many of the things they advocate have been tried and found wanting. Democracy in the classroom, integrated studies, the teacher as a nonauthoritarian figure, creativity as free expression —these and many more of the shibboleths of the romantics were raised widely in American schools from the 1920's through the 1950's. My own conviction is that these ideas have had in the past a deleterious effect on academic achievement and student morale, and that the present effort to make them again dominant is a retrogressive move.

One is struck in reading the romantics (not only those represented in this volume) with their search for perfectability. They are unhappy that social institutions, including schools, reflect the frustrations, compromises, and restraints of the individuals who make up the institutions. Because schools are not the voluntary, noncoercive centers of innocence and pleasure Illich and Goodman want them to be, they must be scrapped. This is an attitude now quite prevalent among the young, and the not-so-young, evident not only in thinking about education but also in thinking about government, business, and the church. It is a sort of philosophical anarchism, akin to Rousseau's notion that man would be naturally good if he were not corrupted by society's arrangements. The notion that the way to improve our lot is to abolish our institutions is, in my view, Utopian, sentimental, and the ultimate cop-out.

Although I have never thought of Carl Bereiter as being one of the romantic radicals, his remarks about teachers in "A Time to Experiment with Alternatives to Education," which appears in this volume, suggest that he, too, may be moving in the direction of educational perfectability. How, he complains, can we achieve sound universal education when there is a notorious shortage of natural teachers? But isn't this true of all of our institutions—this shortage of high talent? There are not enough natural doctors to go around, either, or natural lawyers or editorial writers.

It is inevitable that we have to operate society's institutions with a few geniuses, a goodly number of competent practitioners, many who are mediocre or downright incompetent, and a great middle body of ordinary people who with application can learn some of the rudiments of their calling. We cannot do away with the law because every lawyer is not Sir Edward Coke, abolish theaters because every actor is not Gielgud, refuse to listen to violin playing unless the performer ranks with Issac Stern. It is nonsense to imply that in teaching it must be Comenius and Mark Hopkins or nothing. It is this either-or aspect of the romantic argument that makes one despair of any practical good coming out of the debates the radicals have started.

I find more to agree with in the paper prepared by Everett Reimer than in those of Illich and Goodman. I accept the statement that the relatively low priority accorded to cognitive education "accounts in considerable part for the high costs and low student achievement characteristic of most schools." It is probably true, as the Reimer paper states, that students would be better off if they spent less time in school, if they were subject to fewer tests, and if their schools were less elaborate. I question the assumption, implicit in both Reimer's and Illich's papers, that their studies of education in Puerto Rico and Latin America can produce conclusions that will to any appreciable degree be valid for education in the United States.

I said at the beginning of these comments that I believe some useful reforms can be accomplished within the present framework of the schools. The necessity for brevity limits me to giving four examples. First, I think the schools can, and indeed must, find more efficient ways of teaching the essential first skill, reading. Second, we must find better ways of training and certifying teachers. Third, we need more critical evaluation, in practice, of the many innovations that have been foisted on the schools in recent years. And last, there is an imperative need for higher aspirations in education for children of the ghetto.

I take it that our critics would not entirely agree with either the necessity for the above reforms or the possibility of achieving them. For instance, while thousands of teachers and parents search for effective ways to teach reading, Paul Goodman's contribution is to tell us blithely that any normal child will "pick up the (reading) code unless he is systematically interrupted and discouraged, for instance by trying to teach him in school." Ivan Illich is going to cure the headache of teacher training and certification by decapitation. I think we need to reform teacher certification, not abolish it. My objection to certification as presently constituted (dominated, that is, by the professional, rather than the academic side) is that it tends to certify the shadow and not the substance of the teacher's art. Just as I want a doctor whose training has been primarily in medicine rather than bedside manner, so do I want a mathematics teacher whose training has been primarily in mathematics, not classroom management. We need how-to-do-it preparation, too, but one must learn content before method.

Everett Reimer says the school system fails in its attempt to educate most students of the lower class and suggests that given the present organization of schools, the failure is inevitable. I think the failure arises from the fact that too many schoolmen think the child of the big-city slums is ineducable or take the sociological view that schools cannot accomplish much until the community and the home change. I do not subscribe to this educational determinism because I know of so-called ghetto schools where children *are* achieving—achieving because they are treated humanely and are assumed to be capable of learning.

I must close these random remarks on a note of pessimism. Fifteen years ago the greatest obstacles to constructive change were the "organization men" of the educational establishment. Due in part to Sputnik and in part to a wave of parental dissatisfaction with the schools, persons largely outside the establishment forced many promising curricular changes in the 1960's. Now the modest successes of that period are threatened by the Utopian revolutionaries who tell us society has to be remade (according to their personal blueprint, of course) before education can be improved. I think their demands for perfected human relationships and social arrangements have so diverted and confused the educational debate that the prospects for realizable reform are getting bleaker day by day.

VIII

An Impractical Proposal

Peter H. Wagschal

Like so many other suggestions for the overhaul of American education, the deschool proposal seems to me to be rapidly sinking in the mud and mire of what I can best label as "premature pragmatism." The very idea of eliminating schools from a society as complex as twentieth century America has not been considered with any degree of thoughtfulness for more than two or three years, and yet advocates and critics alike are already quibbling over minute details in the practical realm of "what would a deschooled society look like, exactly?"

It is a typically American reaction, for we are above all else a Pragmatic People. No doubt if Moses had offered a Promised Land to a group of Americans, they would have wanted to see the completed blueprints, including cost-analysis of the sewage system, before they would have reacted positively or negatively to the idea. There is simply something deep in the American character that hungers for practicality and rationality. To put it another way, we are not a society prone to taking huge, imaginative leaps of faith. When we make decisions about the future, we want to *know* the results of those decisions long before they happen and, preferably, before we make the decisions.

Call it pragmatism; call it a need to control the future; call it rationality; call it what you will, this urge runs deep in the American mind (and in all of Western culture, for that matter), tainting whatever it touches. Thus, when a few well-meaning and, I believe, clear-thinking persons suggest the deschooling of American society, the arguments that ensue predictably fall in the realm of practicality.

Predictably and, I think, most unfortunately, the notion of deschooling should raise a host of challenging questions in the realms of values, attitudes, world-views, goals, and beliefs—not particularly pragmatic questions, to be sure, but nevertheless the kind which might well be more important to America in the 1970's than thousands of disputes over the "practicality" of some new educational fad.

Lest the readers of this volume lose sight of the larger (impractical) questions which deschooling raises, I wish to set some of them down here, but before I do so, I must make one thing clear: I consider myself an advocate of deschooling. I would *like* to live in an America which eliminated school as an institution. But, please, do not ask me to spell out in grandiose detail what that deschooled world will be like. I honestly do not know. Nor, I would add, does anyone else, inasmuch as it has not happened yet. My predilection for deschooling is *not* based on either an ESP or computer-aided glimpse of the future. It *is* based on certain values, ideals, and beliefs that I hold which mesh much more comfortably with the philosophy of deschooling than with the operating philosophy of American education as it is. It is simply not a practical matter for me yet, and it will not become one until (or unless) America starts deschooling herself. For me, right now, in a very "schooled" America, deschooling is no more, *and no less,* than an idea, a conception, a world-view. And it is on that level, it seems to me, that it can most fruitfully be discussed—pragmatism to the contrary notwithstanding. But, perhaps, my position will become more clear through a brief look at a few of the many questions legitimately raised by the deschooling controversy.

Whom, or What, Do You Trust?   A society as complex and institutionalized as ours cannot, I think, be said to trust any person in particular, nor does it seem to trust humanity in general. The institutions are there to protect people from each other and from themselves. If there is trust, it is in society and its institutions, but not in human beings per se. Society's basic world-view revolves around a sort of Hobbesian fear of man, who makes it at all only because of the wondrous institutions that keep him from his "nasty, brutish, and short" natural condition.

Educational institutions, of course, epitomize this distrust of both man and the single man. It is the school that knows what, how, and when all students should learn. Neither students nor teachers are in any position to change the curriculum or very much else about the institutional rules that make up the schools.

Any proposal that school be abolished is a challenge to this basic pattern of trust and distrust. To remove the school as authority on what, how, and when people shall learn is to suggest that individual human beings, or perhaps groups of them, can and should make those decisions. It is, in effect, to propose that we all change our attitudes, beliefs, values, and world-views in such a way that we learn to trust ourselves and our fellow human beings instead of the institutions that we now worship.

Again, without wishing to be too repetitive, let me point out that I do not see this as a pragmatic matter. The "trust question" raised by the deschooling proposal is *not* a practical issue resolved by finding out whether students learn more when they are trusted than when not. It is a more basic human issue resolved only by a leap of faith. Do you trust people or do you trust institutions?

Maximum Diversity or Maximum Efficiency?   If nothing else, institutionalized education has the promise of being efficient. That is, whatever it is that schools succeed in imparting to students, the more securely entrenched and institutionalized those schools are, the more efficiently can they impart it. As the American educational system gets larger and larger (in expenditure and personnel) and as it gets more and more standardized, it applauds itself by noting how literate the American people are. The large educational institution's major appeal, in fact, is its claim to efficiency—its ability to "educate" more people at a higher level than a more fragmented, uninstitutionalized process could.

To deschool America would, of course, be enormously inefficient. In fact, to propose deschooling is to suggest that the educational process should not strive to be efficient. It is to suggest that the demands of the learner, rather than the needs of "society" be the foundation of what educational experiences are available, and any school system that actually responds to student demands is bound to be maximally inefficient.

But it is also bound to foster the maximum amount of diversity —in students' interests, skills, personalities, and even life styles— than is possible within the society as a whole. What the schooled society loses in its search for efficiency is diversity. As more students are run through the same educational mill, the differences between subcultures and individuals become smaller. While, on the other hand, as soon as the institutionalized school disappears, to be replaced by small units responding to the needs, and even whimsies, of individual students, a maximum amount of diversity can be fostered and efficiency tossed to the winds. The deschooled society could not brag about how many people learn to read so quickly, but it could boast that all three of the five-year-olds in the country who wanted to learn integral calculus were able to do so.

Again, this is no practical issue. I prefer a deschooled society because diversity fits more with my notions of what human beings are and of what I would like them able to become. And I would willingly cast efficiency aside for those currently untapped human resources.

<u>Curiosity or Pie-in-the-Sky-When-You-Die?</u> In its Hobbesian distrust of man, the school believes him to be a basically lazy animal who needs to be "motivated" by things outside himself if he is ever to do anything worthwhile. The school's whole ladder of grades-certificates-degrees (not to mention society's ladders of money and prestige) is rooted in this view of man as an animal that must be prodded and pulled. Our predominant view of ourselves seems to be that we would either sleep our lives away or engage in all sorts of bad things were it not for the fact that society and its institutions are constantly dangling future rewards in our faces as a prod to stir us into more rewarding and beneficial activities. Who would ever want to learn grammar if the school didn't require it?

To propose, on the other hand, that schools be eliminated is to suggest that man is not quite so lethargic and nasty as inherently and inwardly curious and motivated; that he needs no carrot or stick to move him; that, thrown into a world full of things and beings, he will strive from within to understand and act in that world to the highest of his capabilities.

Insofar as we see ourselves as empty beings, moving only as we are pulled and pushed by the rewards of the outside world, we will continue to have a fondness for schools. But insofar as we see a wealth of life inside ourselves reaching out to the world and constantly seeking to expand, we will see the school and its carrots only an obstacle to that expansion. It is a matter of our basic conception of ourselves, and not a practical question resolved by psychologists "proving" that man is or is not internally motivated.

<u>Stability and Planned Change or Evolution?</u> To return from whence I began, the American character is deeply rational and pragmatic. It tends to hold onto what it has in the present unless a detailed program of change toward a meticulously painted better future is available. We are willing to change ourselves or our institutions only when reason so dictates, and then only if we know exactly what we are changing to and how we will get there.

To suggest that we deschool ourselves is, on the other hand, to urge a leap into the unknown. Eliminate the school and, despite whatever hunches any of us may have about the results, we enter upon a new, unpredictable era. Who knows what things would be like without institutionalized schools? No one. The educational patterns, and even the society, that would result from deschooling would have to *evolve* from what is now to a future that none of us can see. Those of us whose world-views value such evolution and risk-taking will, thus, be inclined to favor deschooling, whereas the more rational among us will hedge at the prospect of so uncontrollable and unpredictable a change.

<u>Deschooling as a World-View Question</u>   The list of questions could go on extensively, but the important point is that they all focus on attitudes, beliefs, values, and world-views rather than on practical considerations. Or, to put it another way, the contrast between advocates and critics of deschooling is a contrast in philosophies of life more than a clash between those who want schools and those who do not. There are those of us who advocate trust in man, the fostering of diversity, a belief in man's innate curiosity, and a propensity for risky, unpredictable, evolutionary change. And, there are others of us who advocate trust in institutions, the development of more efficient schools, a belief that man needs external motivation, and a predilection for planned, rational, controlled change.

Most importantly, it is a mistake to suggest that deschooling can meaningfully take place in the context of the second cluster of attitudes mentioned above. As I see it, at least, it is self-contradictory to advocate deschooling while, at the same time, hoping that we will all continue to trust institutions, like efficiency, believe in man's basic laziness, and seek after controlled, rational change. If the deschooling controversy is going to have any valuable impact on American education, it will be in the realm of the values and ideals or not at all. Otherwise, I am afraid it will go the way of so many of the other legitimate counter-cultural American reform movements, from Dewey right up through Gestalt Therapy—pragmatized to death.

If there is a revolution brewing in America these days, and if deschooling is a part of that revolution, then it is in the realm of our most basic world-view—of what we believe and act on as the nature of man and his world. For America to successfully deschool itself will first require a massive change in attitude, *followed* by whatever practical changes seem appropriate to that new perspective. Should the practical changes come first, as has happened so often in the past and as seems to be happening again with the deschooling movement, then we will have missed another revolution and will have succeeded once again in hanging onto the old, worn-out clothes by changing the signs on the closet.

IX

Prophets and
Scientists in Education

Robert J. Havighurst

Confusion abounds concerning schools and colleges and how well they are serving the modern, highly productive technological society. There is equal questioning and uncertainty about the functions and the effectiveness of formal educational institutions in underdeveloped and developing countries.

Authors seem destined to have a big readership if they write under titles like *Murder in the Schoolroom, Our Children Are Dying, Why the Schools Are Failing, The Death of Higher Education, Compulsory Miseducation.* This caters to a widespread concern on the part of parents as well as many educators about the effectiveness of contemporary schooling and about the aims of formal education.

There are two quite different roles that may be taken by serious critics of contemporary education. One is that of the prophet; the other is that of the scientist. The prophet is primarily concerned with *change* because he believes the present situation is *wrong.* The scientist is primarily concerned with *truth* which he thinks is likely to bring about *change.*

Both of these roles are useful ones. The prophet's criticisms and urge toward reform are much needed at this critical time. And the continuous search for facts about education and human development will provide the basis for improvement of educational practice.

It is a dangerous matter, though, when the two roles are confused. The reader who wants to understand the educational situation and to reach some clear conclusions about educational policy or practice may be confused or misled by a prophet who attempts to assume the role of the scientist. And the same reader may be confused by the scientist who drops this role and becomes a prophet.

The essays we are examining in this book are essentially prophetic. They are written by men with varying degrees of scientific competence who adopt the primary role of the prophet but do not clearly signal this fact to the reader; they tend to draw upon science in a very inadequate and dangerous way. This throws on the reader the responsibility of separating the prophecy from the pseudoscience.

The Scientist. The stereotype of the scientist as the cold, impersonal fact machine has been examined critically and found to be somewhat misleading, whether applied to natural scientists or to social scientists. Their personalities and their personal interests affect their scientific work. The uses to which science is put, the problems which the scientist studies, are largely determined by the values and the goals of the society that supports scientific work. In that sense science is not value-free.

But there are some criteria of good scientific work, and they are continually being applied to scientific studies in the field of education. The scientist is under obligation to tell the truth, and the whole truth, as he sees it. Every proposition he states as a result of his work must be *hammered out on the anvil of established fact.* As a protection for this basic principle of scientific quality, there is the practice of replication. A scientist replicates his own work to be sure of it. Other scientists replicate his work if they have any doubt about it at all.

An example of this test is the attempt by several people to replicate the "Pygmalion experiment" of Rosenthal and Jacobson. Several other investigators repeated the experiment with various groups of children and teachers and failed to confirm the Rosenthal and Jacobson findings.(1) Thus the Pygmalion study has not satisfied scientific criteria.

The Prophet. The prophet operating in the field of education has two very important and useful functions: he points the way toward new educational practices and policies, and he serves as a gadfly, stimulating people to think seriously about the problems of education and to see what is wrong with contemporary education.

Just now the prophets are relatively popular. They appeal to the undefined frustration and discontent of thoughtful people who are convinced that we should make sweeping changes in our society, including our educational system.

It is important for students and practitioners of education to listen to prophets and learn from them but to remember that they are prophets and not scientists. Their approach to truth is that of the prophet, not that of the scientist.

It is also important to recognize the fact that there are false prophets as well as true prophets. The distinction between the false and the true prophet is not clear. It does not lie in their success or failure to predict the future—to prophesy, in that sense of the word; it lies in their ability to grasp social reality and interpret it to people in terms of their own needs and aspirations. The distinction between true and false also lies in the ability to evaluate the possibilities for peaceful social change and to weigh these possibilities against those of violent revolution, with its resulting social improvement. It lies in the social and ethical values they espouse.

Deschooling—an Elitist Concept. The most serious difficulty with the proposals for deschooling is that they favor the *haves* against the *have-nots*. They are elitist, in spite of the fact that some of their proponents argue for deschooling as though they believed it would give greater opportunity to poor people and their children.

The social group that could give their children the best education in a society without schools is the well-to-do group that could both employ tutors for their children and teach their children informally in the family. Free public schooling was invented in democratic countries to give greater opportunity to economically disadvantaged children and adults. It has succeeded in this to some extent, as is proven by the numbers of poor children who have become quite successful workers, citizens, and parents at least partly with the aid of schools. Of course, no one who dislikes poverty and racial and economic discrimination is satisfied with the degree of opportunity in modern democratic societies. But those who try to work to improve the educational institutions as conveyors of opportunity are on a sounder course, in the judgment of this writer, than those who want to abolish the existing educational institutions.

Ivan Illich. Like other prophets, Ivan Illich is a man of an intense moral fervor—a moral fervor which shows itself frequently as a burning hatred of the social institutions of affluent democracies and their attempts to influence and "aid" the poor and underdeveloped countries. Born in Central Europe, Illich grew up in Vienna and became a Catholic priest. Emigrating to the United States, he was assigned to a Puerto Rican parish in New York City. He served the parish with such skill and devotion that he was sent to Puerto Rico, where he became vice-rector of the Catholic University at Ponce. From that post he left active service for the church and moved to Mexico, where he founded the Centro Intercultural de Documentacion in Cuernavaca, a center for study and publication of sociocultural information about Latin America. Since 1967, that center has held seminars and conferences and issued publications aimed at a radical reconstruction of school systems.

Ivan Illich has looked critically at two quite different educational systems—that of Latin America and that of the United States. His critiques are different since one educational system operates in an underdeveloped economy characterized by deep poverty of masses of people and a tradition of aristocratic rule, while the other educational system is a product of the wealthiest society, with a tradition of democratic government. In both critiques he is useful as a gadfly, but misleading as one who is supposed to be reporting accurately and making positive proposals for improvement.

The depth of Illich's aversion to schools cannot be stated secondhand. One must read his words to sense it. All the evils of human society seem to be wrapped up in the institution of the school, which is evil wherever it is found.

In a basic sense, schools have ceased to be dependent on the ideology professed by any government or market organization. Other basic institutions might differ from one country to another: family, party, church, or press. But everywhere the school system has the same structure, and everywhere its hidden curriculum has the same effect.(2)

The escalation of the schools is as destructive as the escalation of weapons but less visibly so.(3)

The safeguards of individual freedom are all cancelled in the dealings of a teacher with his pupil.(4)

Illich sees the evil of the school as impervious to reform.
". . . to hope for fundamental change within the school system as an effect of conventionally conceived social or economic change is also an illusion.(5)

In his long essay on "The Futility of Schooling in Latin America," which was given wide circulation by *Saturday Review,* (6) he starts with the gross error of writing about Latin America as though it were all of a piece, when every scholar of Latin American society distinguishes clearly between at least three groups of countries, which are as different in their social structures and educational systems as England and Greece. At the more developed end of the scale are Argentina, Chile, Uruguay, Cuba, and Puerto Rico; while the least developed group consists of Ecuador, Bolivia, Guatamala, Santo Domingo, San Salvador, and Nicaragua. The middle group consists of Brazil, Peru, Colombia, and Venezuela. Brazil, with one-third of the population of Latin America, shows more difference in educational level, literacy, and per capita income between the southern and northern states of São Paulo and Maranhão than that between New York and Mississippi.

Illich claims that the school system in Latin America offers the only legitimate passage for poor children to the middle class, and that this system "remains closed to the masses." Both parts of this claim are false. Numerous studies have shown that many young people have moved from lower-class to middle-class status with very little schooling. For instance, a study of technicians made in Brazil in 1962 showed that 21 percent of the people who held technician level jobs (lower-middle class) had no more than the Brazilian four-year primary school education. With respect to Illich's statement that the school system "remains closed to the masses," this writer's study of a large sample of middle-school students (equivalent to the North American high school) from a wide range of Brazilian states showed that 22 percent of the graduating class came from homes of the manual working class.(7)

Reimer in his new book entitled *School Is Dead* says, "Two thirds of all children in Latin America leave school before finishing the fifth grade."(8) Illich says, "No more than one percent graduate from a university."(9) The fact is that in Chile, Argentina, Uruguay, Southern Brazil, Costa Rica, Mexico, and Cuba, at least 50 percent of an age group get at least six years of schooling. More than 1 percent graduate from a university in Argentina, Uruguay, and the southern half of Brazil, showing a higher university graduation rate than most of the Mediterranean countries of Europe.

To be sure, educational opportunity is less in Latin America, even in the more developed countries, than it should be. But Illich's technique is to ascribe the worst-appearing facts falsely to all of Latin America, and then to ask for revolutionary changes in all of Latin America. There is no concreteness to his proposals for educational change in Latin America, except for his approval of the personal methods of Paulo Freire in teaching illiterate adults, methods which have not been adapted to more general use by other educators.

I favor an extension of Freire's methods, if this proves practicable, and also the liberal political measures of social and land reform which Illich's writing would imply that he also favors. But I would opt for systematic extension of the free and obligatory school system, which is not nearly as costly as Illich suggests.

Illich's devastating critique of the modern affluent society is useful. This modern Jeremiah denounces the senseless overconsumption of material goods by the wealthy societies, their greed for material things, and their tendency to overorganize the lives of people. But Illich's proposals for new and "revolutionary" educational procedures, described in his book on deschooling, are feeble and lifeless. This is probably Illich's last word on education. His first attempt to be constructive may be his last. Probably he will resume the role of prophet, with prophetic and useful critiques of other aspects of modern life.

Illich's piece on deschooling is an example of both the strength and the weakness of the prophet. The prophet is good at pointing to the faults and the wrongs of the society. But he is not good at repairing the society or constructing a better society.

<u>Reimer-Illich Alternatives.</u>   Mr. Reimer appears to be the realist of Cuernavaca. He is the one who proposes practical procedures. His voice is more moderate, more practical, less prophetic, than the other voices from Cuernavaca. His proposals for alternatives to schools are stated in simple language, and he attempts to take account of objections to them. In the Cuaderno 1001 of 1970, he begins to describe alternatives to schools. One can only ask the knowledgeable reader to study them carefully. In my opinion they suffer from the elitism mentioned earlier. The parents and the adults who are already successful would make the best use of these alternatives, both for their children and for themselves.

In the Cuaderno 1005 (1971), Reimer undertakes to put some reality into Illich's proposal for four educational networks to take the place of schools. This undertaking is not reported in the present volume, and it should not be prejudged. I have not yet read Reimer's 1971 material, though I have heard some oral reporting on the subject. What the Reimer-Illich team will have to do is to demonstrate how these four educational networks can serve disadvantaged children and their parents as well as or better than a system of schools and other institutions based on the present system when this system is substantially improved with the improvements that are visible and have been tested and proven effective.

The weaknesses of Illich's four educational networks are evident on careful reading, and will only be mentioned briefly.
1) "Reference Services to Educational Objects." A wide variety of educational materials would be stored and catalogued in tool shops, laboratories, libraries, and gaming rooms for use by students of all ages. Students who were qualified would have access to these materials, even if they were being used by factories in production.

   Admitting the educational values of young people studying and working with these materials, it is clear that the families with the fullest acquaintance with and grasp of these educational objects could make the most effective use of them—and not the poor and disadvantaged families.
2) "Skill Exchanges." People with valuable skills which they are willing to teach to others would be listed in a skill exchange. Such people as nurses, specialists in foreign language, technicians, accountants, and computer programmers, would make their services available as teachers. Students would receive

vouchers from the government which would entitle them to go to tutors and seek instruction. Again, it is clear that the parents who are themselves most successful and sophisticated would help their children find the best tutors.

3) Peer Matching. Students would be helped to find other students with similar educational interests and needs. They would be aided by an information exchange to form small or large groups for learning purposes.

The problem of the illiterate and inexperienced parent becomes clear when one considers the amount of knowledge this parent would need to command in order to do a good job of "peer matching" for his children. The essentially middle-class character of Illich's proposal to use a computer for the purposes of peer matching becomes clear when one tries to imagine a working-class, ghetto-dwelling mother trying to fig-ure out how to use the computer to match her ten-year-old son and her fifteen-year-old daughter with peers in a variety of learning activities.

4) "Reference Services to Educators-at-Large." Somebody would make a directory "giving the addresses and self-descriptions of professionals, paraprofessionals, and freelancers, along with conditions of access to their services. Such educators . . . could be chosen by polling or consulting their former clients." This is very similar to the skill exchange mentioned earlier. Presumably, this listing would take the place of the teacher's certificate as an indicator of the instructor's competence and character, and students could choose their teachers. The in-dependent educator would replace the teacher assigned to a classroom, waiting for students that were assigned to him or her.

5) Conclusions. In this laissez faire, free enterprise system of edu-cation, the four networks would have to be designed and operated by somebody, "but not in the numbers or the type required by the administration of schools," according to Illich. "Student discipline, public relations, hiring, supervising, and firing teachers would have neither place nor counterpart in the networks I have been describing."

It seems likely, as Illich and Reimer indicate, that the number of people involved in operating the educational institutions as cer-tified teachers, counselors, and administrators would decrease, and the number and variety of persons serving as guides and models and instructors would increase. This would have the initial advan-tage of freeing the educational system of some of the bureaucratic rigidity and inefficiency that always develops in a bureaucracy.

But it is impossible for this writer to understand how the children and adults and communities who need education most could get a fair deal in this kind of nonsystem. On the contrary, those who are best able to take care of their own education would make the best use of the four networks, while those disadvantaged by illiteracy and poverty would be neglected. Eventually, people with a social conscience would work through political and economic measures to set up educational institutions to serve the disadvantaged people better, and a school system would emerge again, as it did in the nineteenth century in the present developed countries.

Carl Bereiter. Carl Bereiter's "think piece" for the congressional committee on education represents an interesting stage in the development of the educational philosophy of this highly creative young man. He has been criticized by the humanists for his emphasis on *training the minds* of children, especially disadvantaged children. The method he and Siegfried Engelmann developed at the University of Illinois was described by one popular writer as a "pressure cooker for young minds."

In this recent piece he appears to hold to his earlier emphasis on training the mind, but to define its scope in a limited way—limited to the teaching of basic mental skills, which he says can be done effectively with one-third of the time and money now devoted to elementary and secondary schooling. His major suggestion is to:

"Restrict the responsibility of the schools entirely to training in well-defined, clearly teachable skills. This would require only about a third of the cost in money, personnel, and time that schooling costs now. What would be lost would be largely good riddance, and with exclusive concentration on training, the schools could probably do a much more efficient and pleasing job of it than they do now.

To meet needs for humanistic education, Bereiter asks that society provide funds to "support the development of new kinds of cultural opportunities for children, to take the place of schooling."

As Bereiter develops his ideas about education during the next years, it will be interesting to see how he relates himself to the anarchistic deschooling group in which he appears to find himself at this moment.

Paul Goodman. Paul Goodman is the most urbane of the deschoolers. He is more sophisticated about educational institutions and about human nature, and he is more skeptical of the revolutionary aspect of the counterculture. As a follower of Rousseau and a self-styled anarchist, Goodman makes it clear at all times that he wants to minimize the force of institutions in society and to keep the individual as free as possible from the chains of custom and of law. His five propositions sum this up.(10)

Goodman's proposal for a system of mini-schools for ages six to eleven would produce, in a city of one million, about 4,000 separate schools, each with a staff of four: 1) A teacher licensed and salaried as in the present system. Since the present average class size is twenty-eight, these are available; 2) A graduating college senior from one of the local colleges, perhaps embarking on graduate study. Salary $2000. There is no lack of candidates, young people who want to do something useful and interesting in a free setting; 3) A literate housewife and mother, who can also prepare lunch. Salary $4000. Again there is no lack of candidates; 4) A literate, willing, and intelligent high school graduate or dropout. Salary $2000. No lack of candidates.(11)

The minute Goodman starts to think about this, in realistic terms, it becomes more complicated and more institutionalized. He says:

For its setting, the mini-school would occupy two, three, or four rooms in existing school buildings or church basements and settlement houses otherwise empty during school hours, rooms set aside in housing built by public funds, and rented storefronts. The layout is fairly indifferent, since a major part of activity would occur outside the place. . . .(12)

I can think of nothing more interesting than to see the elementary schools of a city of one million changed into a set of mini-schools for an experimental period of five or ten years. Since there would have to be at least a small central administration, we would hope that Paul Goodman would accept the superintendency, or at least someone nominated and advised by him.

The advantages would appear most clearly in perhaps one hundred of the four thousand mini-schools that would be needed. These would be schools sponsored by groups of liberal parents who would organize themselves so as to get what they regarded as a good "mix" in terms of race and income and would quickly absorb the available supply of teachers possessing the competence and maturity to operate such a school.

One wonders how Superintendent Goodman or his lieutenants in the central office would handle the following all-too-likely situations:

1) A telephone call concerning the three children aged six, eight, and ten of an ADC mother who is herself illiterate and burdened with two smaller children. She has not found a mini-school in her neighborhood, and she telephones the central office or the district office for help.

2) The police report that a number of ten- and eleven-year-old boys are forming a local neighborhood gang which hides out in an abandoned building that is slated for urban renewal. When asked about school, the boys say they cannot find one. At the nearest mini-school, teachers say they cannot cope with the behavior of these boys.

3) The alderman of a ward composed largely of hard-hat white workers presents a petition for the restoration of the local public school, where there will be some "discipline," the children will be kept off the streets, and the parents will know who is boss of the school their children attend. The former school principal would be reinstated.

4) The parents' committee in charge of a school report to the central office that they suspect the woman who acts as cook and housemother is keeping some of the money she gets to purchase food and housekeeping utensils for the school, either through a kick back arrangement with a local grocer or through falsifying her records.

These hypothetical situations are meant to suggest that the administration of 4,000 mini-schools may require a bureaucracy as complicated and as expensive to the city as the former administration of 150 elementary schools.

To turn to another problem raised by what may be too simplistic a concept of the educational process, Goodman and other critics are fond of citing what they perceive as the analogy between learning to speak and learning to read. Goodman says, "The analogy between learning to speak and learning to read is not exact, but it is instructive to pursue it, since, in principle, speaking should be much harder to pick up."(13) The reader might look critically at Goodman's discussion of this analogy and analyze his conclusion that it is possible and feasible to teach reading somewhat in the way children learn to speak—by intrinsic interest, with personal attention, and in a lifelike environment. A number of intelligent and serious researchers have studied the process of learning to read, and they fail to see much of an analogy between learning to read and learning to speak. Only in a middle-class family are the rewards and punishments involved in learning or not learning to read at something like the level of those that apply to talking. The argument has some validity for middle-class children but very little for children brought up in the culture of poverty.

Here, as elsewhere, Goodman and other critics display an unconscious elitism that is one of the basic faults of their ideology. The result of their proposals would be to favor the families who are already educated and know what they want for their children and to penalize the poor and the ignorant.

Notes

1. Robert Rosenthal and Lenore Jacobson. *Pygmalion in the Classroom* (New York: Holt, Rinehart and Winston, 1968). See also J. D. Elashoff and Richard Snow. *Pygmalion Reconsidered* (Worthington, Ohio: Charles A. Jones Publishing Company, 1972).

2. Ivan Illich. *DeSchooling Society* (New York: Harper & Row, 1971) p. 74.
3. Ibid., p. 10.
4. Ibid., p. 31.
5. Ibid., p. 74.
6. Ivan Illich. "The Futility of Schooling in Latin America," *Saturday Review* (April 20, 1968), pp. 57-59, 74-75.
7. Robert J. Havighurst and Aparecida Gouveia. *Brazilian Secondary Education and Socioeconomic Development* (New York: Praeger, 1969).
8. Everett Reimer, *School is Dead* (New York: Doubleday & Company, 1971) p. 7.
9. Ivan Illich. Ibid., p. 59.
10. Paul Goodman. *The New Reformation: Notes of a Neolithic Conservative* (New York: Randon House, 1970), pp. 85-86.
11. Ibid., pp. 97-98.
12. Ibid., p. 98.
13. Ibid., p. 92.

X

The Educational Mission

Amitai Etzioni

The four contributions before us reflect the current stance toward educational institutions. All four are broadly rebellious: they view the contemporary system of education as highly counterproductive, as not only failing to serve its purposes but as causing severe damage. These four authors, given the choice of pushing a button to eliminate the existing system of education, would do so—though with varying degrees of reluctance, or, I should say, dispatch.

On the face of it, all four authors, as well as many other educationalist critics, seem seriously engaged in transformation. It is the main point of my commentary, however, that while the basic charges the rebellion makes against the existing system are valid (although the criticism is often too sweeping and exaggerated), the business of transformation is yet to be given serious attention. The critics, I would argue, are typically ultraoptimistic about human nature and excessively Utopian about the possibilities of casting new societal patterns. If the critical fire is to generate more guiding light for the forthcoming transformation of our educational system and society, its bearers must become more realistic, empirical, and in this sense, more relevant.

The particular way in which an author, critic, or (by implication) an institution sees human nature is the corner stone on which the intellectual tower rests. The present school system, or, more precisely, its worst parts, tends to assume (not necessarily consciously but as suggested by its institutional structure) that the child is a wild beast who must be civilized. Hence a large segment of school life is disciplinary, aimed at keeping the lid on and training the child to sit still, listen, obey, and absorb information, skills, and values.

The critics see a quite different child. They believe that the child, by nature, is eager to learn. If his nature is allowed to unfold, free from the distorting effects of the school, he will take to education like a sunflower to sunshine. Illich thus argues that "we can depend on self-motivated learning instead of employing teachers to bribe or compel the student to find time and the will to learn." The child may need help to be sufficiently motivated, help a motivated and well-guided teacher may provide without bribe or force but by use of positive models and symbolic rewards.

It is the exceedingly optimistic assumption that the child is self-propelling, which allows the rebellion to pass as transformation—in the guise of reductionism. This deserves some elaboration. The main suggestion endorsed by all four authors, albeit in varying degrees, is that the amount and scope of schooling must be drastically reduced in order to "free" education from its institutional cage. By and large, school is not to be replaced by anything. Education is to occur chiefly by itself, by the child's participation in *on-going* activities and his selection of which set of resources he will apply to himself. This position has two attributes: first, it suggests that by merely doing away with institutions (a position taken elsewhere vis-à-vis sexual taboos and authority), we not only eliminate the existing system but also provide a viable foundation for the new world. Second, it frees the analyst from having to think out what new system will have to be erected—the child knows best where he should be and what he needs. Practically all the specific suggestions made here are based on this double assumption: the child wishes to learn and he needs less, not more, institutional support. Goodman's notion of incidental learning, Bereiter's and Illich's notion of providing the child with educational resources, and the shared view of the teacher as a child's "source person," all assume that the child is able *and* motivated to learn and that his choices are the educated and educating ones.

The evidence in favor of those cheerful assumptions is slim and very difficult to evaluate. A review of the data and the methodological difficulties involved is a task we cannot undertake here.* However, two points can be made, drawing not on empirical data but on the logic of the arguments involved. First, educational institutions are clearly part of the societal web. The child, even if he "naturally" would have been education-eager, obviously does not enter school unaffected by his family, his neighborhood, the mass media, etc. Obviously he was exposed to these influences *before* he was of school age, and they also continue to affect him while he is at school. By and large, these forces are similar to the *old* school system—they tend to make the child passive, dependent, alienated.

---

*See Amitai Etzioni, *The Active Society* (New York: The Free Press, 1968; paperback edition, 1971), chap. 21.

The question hence must be raised: What child do the optimists talk about—the postrevolutionary child, born to a liberated home and community in a society in which all means of production are collectivized, the media are educational, etc.? Or is he the one who is actually entering our schools now? Can he be truly freed simply by releasing him from school? Must we not try to help children— at least until the revolution comes—to overcome the distortions they bring to school from their nonliberated backgrounds? And are not these distortions deep and severe enough to require a teacher and a school which can motivate, plan, and guide, rather than relying on the child of a distorted society to supervise his own rehabilitation? Are not children like those workers who have not yet acquired class awareness—in need of resourceful, active, effective leadership and a master educational plan? They will never awake from their TV-induced, parent-supported slumber if they follow Goodman's prescription:

The goal of elementary education should be a very modest one: it is for a small child, under his own steam, not on a leash, to be able to poke interestedly into whatever goes on and to be able, by observation, questions, and practical imitation, to get something out of it on his own terms.

One answer, of which Illich is a particularly keen proponent, is that education is the realm in which the revolution would be generated. By redoing the child, we set into motion a major force which could redo society. But I find it difficult to see how one can assume that the forces which sustain the existing economic and political stratification and the structures of mass media will allow the educational resources to be used against them. And I am not aware of any evidence that education can be used as a lever to lift the world. I am inclined to hold that education can change along with other institutions, both helping to change them and being helped to change by their change. But education cannot be the prime transformer.

And, if we are to educate children, let us not kid them and ourselves about the scope, depth, and extent of the project involved. Transforming a society is not an ego trip or a love-in. It is not merely a question of changing one's lifestyle but of unlocking millions caught in the psychic, economic, and political tangle of the existing society. Whoever wishes to participate in this enterprise will have to have much of the self-discipline, the commitment to society above self and immediate peers, and the long-run perspective so unpopular among the education rebels.

Thus, for the time being, to eradicate educational institutions is to turn children over to other nonfree institutions, for example, from the authoritarian family to the exploitative labor market. To provide children with educational resources and teachers who respond rather than guide is to assume that children are already liberated, while in fact they must yet be set free. And to assume that there will be an easy transformation of the modern society to a good society is to underestimate greatly the tenacity of modernity and hence the magnitude of the educational and revolutionary mission.

To the Deschoolers

Maxine Greene

Reviewing the novels of Kurt Vonnegut, Jr., for *The New Republic,* Charles Thomas Samuels writes: "To appreciate Vonnegut you have to be preconvinced; this saves the artist from the terrible bother of art." Somewhat the same thing may be said about the proponents of deschooling. You have to be preconvinced that the school "is the major component of the system of consumer production," that it (in every instance) alienates, stultifies, and deforms. At once you have to be preconvinced not only of the value of autonomy and "personal acts," but of the likelihood that a true learning society can be created through the eradication of the public school. The writers are, in that case, saved from "the terrible bother" of logical argument, particularly with respect to their major premises. They can assert, as Ivan Illich does, that "it is an illusion that schools are only a dependent variable." The reason? "Schooling is necessary to produce the habits and expectations of the managed consumer society."

If you are, however, eager to resist the emotive appeal of the new anti-institutionalism, it is important to identify—and to differentiate among—the vantage points involved. Illich is a disestablishmentarian Catholic, with undoubtedly painful recollections of the ways in which a vast and powerful institution can erode personal autonomy. Many of his orientations, moveover, have been toward Latin America and the Third World, as his references to village life and peasant communities testify. The paradoxes and inhumanities associated with modernization seemingly afflict him deeply, as they do Everett Reimer, who has long been similarly engaged with Latin Americans and their plight. From the perspective of "undeveloped" countries, with their ancient cultures and their distinctive time schemes, the overpowering "development" of the

United States understandably makes this nation seem more monolithic, more manipulative, more grimly materialist than it actually is. In any event, it is at least possible that Illich's and Reimer's analyses are affected by this perspective, for all the obvious resemblances to the perspectives of the counter culture, the Marcusians, and those preoccupied by what Jacques Ellul names "technique."

Paul Goodman's vantage point is more widely known. Self-described anarchist, psychologist, linguist, novelist, and poet, he had been long and eloquently concerned with the American system's transformations of vital, hopeful persons into "personnel." His tones are Emersonian when he speaks of the coercive character of institutions, the evils of the "preconceived curriculum," the separation of the schools from life. He becomes Aristotelian when he says that "most people cannot organize their lives without productive activity that is socially approved" and goes on (unlike Illich) to propose apprenticeship programs, innovative community activities, and "schooling (sic.) on the job." Like John Dewey and A. H. Neill (and unlike Carl Bereiter), he proposes that "a protective and life-nourishing environment" be provided for children up through twelve. Despite his interest in incidental learning, his belief that "youth communities" should take over the functions of high schools, and his conviction that adults ought to attend universities after they have entered into their vocations rather than before, Goodman at no point takes what Illich calls the only true "revolutionary" position: he does not argue systematically for the elimination of schools.

Carl Bereiter, a psychologist become famous among educators for the preschool programs he developed at Illinois with Siegfried Engelmann, is only tangentially related to Illich. Experimental and positivistic, he proposes that the schools restrict themselves to "training in well-defined, clearly teachable skills," more than likely according to the model of "pattern drills" used at Illinois. (It may be relevant to quote Bereiter on the "highly disciplined manner" in which instruction is to be carried on in early compensatory education: "The pace is fast," he has written, "all children are required to respond and to put forth continual effort. Guessing and thoughtlessness in responding are discouraged.") His ideas cut across Illich's because of Illich's interest in skill centers and Bereiter's view that the school's responsibility should be limited to skill training, with children set free the rest of the time "to do what they want." But Bereiter gives no evidence of wishing to remake American society. Conceiving humanistic values to be dysfunctional, given the present deficiencies of the teachers, he simply wants to stop the schools from attempting to educate: they are to concentrate on training instead.

These strange bedfellows, going at the matter of schooling from their separate angles, have aroused wide audiences to questioning; and this, in itself, is a contribution. Also, despite their often undocumented assertions and sweeping claims, they are directing attention to the oldest and most cherished American values—those having to do with the rights and powers of the individual. Illich talks of "liberating education," self-motivation, self-creation. Reimer is concerned with providing "optimum conditions for the development of all men's minds." Goodman wants to enhance the individual's power "to learn and cope," to make significant choices, to "meet reality," to find something he or she "is good at and can do." Even Bereiter takes issue with rewards for "correctness and docility" and demands the expansion of "options open to children." And all four, very much in the tradition of John Dewey, define ongoing learning as their objective: the increasing ability of students to become their own teachers, subject to no one's manipulation, to no one's alien will.

To what degree are they innovative? To what degree are they realistic? Is their view of schooling justified? Can their objectives be achieved *only* if society is deschooled? There is nothing particularly new in their general conception of education, if education is equated with growth and thought of as intentional cognitive action on the part of a learner. Nor is there anything particularly new in their notions of resources made available to children in the culture and the neighboring community. The importance of incidental (or concomitant) learning was clear to the progressive educators, as were the dangers of the predetermined curriculum and the isolation of the school from "life." Formalism, academicism, sterility, rigidity, indoctrination—all were identified as harmful long before the advent of romantics and deschoolers. Illich, Reimer, and their associates appear innovative mainly in their use of constructs like "system" and "manipulative society" to promote traditional progressive values.

Illich, of course, narrows the constructs when he decides to characterize this as, above all, a "managed consumer society." Arbitrary though this stipulation may be, it is necessary if he is to go on and present the school system not as a dependent variable, but as the dominant institutional force. This *is,* without a doubt, innovative. Edgar Friedenberg, Bayard Rustin, Peter Schrag, and many others have called the school a "selecting out" agency and talked about its focal role in certifying or grading people. Student radicals have frequently complained about the way educational institutions "process" them to fill ready-made slots in the corporate structure. But no one has ascribed such overwhelming power to the schools, certainly not with the assurance demonstrated in Illich's essay. At most, critics have treated them as functions of, or reflections of, or servants of an inequitable, class-structured, credentials-bound society. In a recent *Daedalus* article, "The History of Education," John E. Talbott shows how little is actually known about the relation between education and social structure at any given moment of time. He writes, for example, that

it is not enough simply to describe with greater precision the role of education in the promotion of social mobility (or in the maintenance of established social positions). It also needs to be asked what the consequences of this form of mobility have been, what it has meant to the individuals who experienced it and the societies in which they lived. Such qualitative questions may be exceedingly difficult to answer.

Illich and Reimer, it would seem, have little difficulty answering them; and it is on the basis of their answers that they develop their conception of reform.

Skill centers, networks for the provision of "equal opportunity for learning and teaching," storefronts stocked with cassettes, peer matching, and the rest are certainly innovative. In Illich's presentation, they seem immensely attractive; indeed, he makes them seem, for all his qualifications, *possible.* He himself, however, has emphasized the society's dependence upon the school system for the production of consumers. Can he really believe that what he calls "consumer resistance" will be sufficient for the abolition of the schools? Can he, knowing the impersonality, disorder, and scale of the city, believe that it can be transformed into a hospitable place for children—an "educational world"? More seriously, can he believe that an "institutional inversion of schools" will be sufficient for a breakthrough where the "ultimate political barriers" are concerned? He says little or nothing about political education or deliberate social action. When he speaks about peer matching and the generally acknowledged fact that urban residents "participate simultaneously in several peer groups," he suggests that the individual's ability to meet with others for the sake of "meaningful conversation" may in time make "creative political exchange" more likely.

How does this confront problems of housing welfare, drug addiction, hunger? How does it insure the emergence of qualified change agents? Illich's answer would be that nothing can be done about these problems so long as people are manipulated by professionals, particularly professionals in the schools. His hope (like that of certain nineteenth century romantic reformers) is tied to the liberation of individuals for "voluntary participation in society through networks which provide access to all its resources for learning."

It follows that the schools are the major obstacles to significant social reform; since those potentially capable of effecting such reform are manipulated into acquiescence by the professionals in the schools. Yet Bereiter emphasizes the lack of talent among these professionals; and Reimer asserts that the school system "fails in its attempt to educate most students of the lower class." If these things are so, what are the grounds for claiming such efficiency in teaching, for example, "socially approved values," the very values that force people into consumer roles and into slots that are predefined? The answer may be (Bereiter to the contrary) that the schools are good at training but not at "educating." *Or* it may be that the only thing they truly do well is keep a particular age group in a condition of dependence merely because that group is compelled to attend school.

Conventional wisdom tells us these days that schools "mutilate," coerce, exert "mindless" controls. The romantic critique, combined with an amount of empirical study, has convinced large sections of the public that classrooms are dull, regimented places where little learning takes place. Docility and meekness are presumably rewarded more often than intellectual initiative. Creativity, according to numerous reports, is considered suspect; questioning is stifled; keeping order (and keeping records) are more important than helping people learn to learn. According to the deschoolers, all this must be purposeful. Unlike Charles Silberman, who attributes it to lack of purpose, they appear to see it as a type of conspiracy carried on in the interests of a managed society.

There are, of course, many other explanations: community parochialism or disinterest; lack of financial support; ineffectual teacher education; the persistence of ancient, unexamined pieties (or "middle-class values" or "racist attitudes"); the tradition of imposing social control by means of the schools. The erosion of trust throughout the culture may play a part; so may the generation gap, the pervasive depersonalization, the feelings of powerlessness, the moral uncertainties, the loss of community, the decline of institutional "legitimacy," the inability to cope with proliferating knowledge.

Any one of these factors may make questionable the continuing viability of the "common school" as traditionally conceived. But an inversion of the system, an all-or-none eradication of all existing schools, does not seem a potent enough remedy for our society's multiple deficiencies. "Junk" is discussed; games are touted; the banning of cars from Manhattan is proposed. But nothing is said about mastery of the disciplines needed to conceptualize technology—or the economic system, or public spending, or city planning, or even the works of art which are to be circulated among people who (too frequently) have never learned to see.

The one obvious result of the arrangements being proposed is, it must be granted, a weakening of "managerial values" as educational determinants, since market demand will scarcely be considered if learning becomes a matter of free choice. Yet this raises another problem, especially where the parents of poor children are concerned. Illich and his associates acknowledge inequities (as who cannot?); they touch lightly upon the need to educate parents with respect to self-motivated learning. They do not, however, deal squarely with the compelling desire of poor persons for schools which *do* effectively meet current market demands. Parents eager for their children's success (even in the present inequitable society) will not be satisfied by reminders that the schools have never overcome economic inequities, that the credentials system will continue to penalize them, that in any case the society is overly manipulative, invalidating by its very nature any attempt to achieve community in the neighborhoods, not to mention community control.

Not only is there an implicit elitism in the arguments of the deschoolers; there is, as well, a fearsome (and paradoxical) lack of confidence in the individual's ability to work within the system, to choose himself as anything but a functionary, a Kafkaesque "clerk." The assumption that the teacher can do nothing within the institutions to arouse students to critical thinking or creative endeavor implies a determinist view with respect to the nature of man. Aware of the weaknesses and injustices in our society, concerned to develop strategies to correct them, we need not—indeed we cannot—give up our faith in the human being's capacity to rebel.

To say, as Bereiter does, that the average teacher is simply not talented enough to live up to the "humanist ideal" is to express a kind of contempt for the individual. To assume that the individual teacher can do nothing but indoctrinate, manipulate, and enforce an alien reality upon the young is to reject human possibility. Also, it is to ignore the theoretical and practical work which has clarified the nature of human development, concept-learning, sense-making in general.

The deschoolers do recognize the potential contribution of pedagogues when they are voluntarily selected and when they are willing to engage others, treated as equals, in shared inquiry. Why cannot the same kinds of people, working within our admittedly fallible schools, put the tools of technology to humane use while engaging other human beings in seeking themselves? How are the mindless and dehumanizing forces presently loose in the culture to be combated, if not by intentional action, intentional choice on the part of those committed to education? *This* is where the "terrible bother" should begin—the bother of liberating teachers *and* students to remake their world.

Related Professional Books from

Cha

Curriculum Improvement for Better Schools, Jack R. Frymier, Ohio State University, and Horace C. Hawn, University of Georgia, 1970.

Behind the Classroom Door, John I. Goodlad, University of California, Los Angeles, M. Frances Klein, Institute for Development of Educational Activities, Inc., and Associates, 1970.

Toward Improved Urban Education, Frank W. Lutz, Editor, Pennsylvania State University, 1970.

The Impact of Negotiations in Public Education: The Evidence from the Schools, Charles R. Perry, University of Pennsylvania, and Wesley A. Wildman, University of Chicago, 1970.

Humanistic Foundations of Education, John Martin Rich, University of Texas, 1971.

Guiding Human Development: The Counselor and the Teacher in the Elementary School, June Grant Shane, Harold G. Shane, Robert L. Gibson, and Paul F. Munger, Indiana University, 1971.

Innovations in Education:Their Pros and Cons, Herbert I. Von Haden, Miami University, and Jean Marie King, Alachua County, Florida, Schools, 1971.

Early Childhood Education: Perspectives on Change, Evelyn Weber, Wheelock College, 1971.

Charles A. Jones Publishing Company
Village Green   698 High Street
Worthington, Ohio 43085